# The 20th Century's

## MOST INFLUENTIAL

## HISPANICS

# Ellen Ochoa

## First Female Hispanic Astronaut

by John F. Wukovits

**LUCENT BOOKS**

*An imprint of Thomson Gale, a part of The Thomson Corporation*

Detroit • New York • San Francisco • New Haven. Conn. • Waterville. Maine • London

# THOMSON

★

## GALE

© 2007 Thomson Gale, a part of The Thomson Corporation.

Thomson and Star Logo are trademarks and Gale and Lucent Books are registered trademarks used herein under license.

For more information, contact:
Lucent Books
27500 Drake Rd.
Farmington Hills, MI 48331-3535
Or you can visit our Internet site at http://www.gale.com

**LIBRARY OF CONGRESS CATALOGING-IN-PUBLICATION DATA**

Wukovits, John F., 1944–
   Ellen Ochoa / by John F. Wukovits.
      p. cm. — (The twentieth century's most influential Hispanics)
Includes bibliographical references and index.
ISBN-13: 978-1-59018-976-4 (hardcover : alk. paper)
ISBN-10: 1-59018-976-0 (hardcover : alk. paper)
1. Ochoa, Ellen—Juvenile literature. 2. Women astronauts—United States—Biography—Juvenile literature. 3. Astronauts—United States—Biography—Juvenile literature. 4. Hispanic American women—Biography—Juvenile literature. I. Title.
TL789.85.O25.W85 2006
629.450092—dc22

                                                                  2006021291

Printed in the United States of America

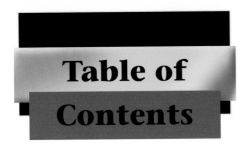

# Table of Contents

# Foreword

When Alberto Gonzales was a boy living in Texas, he never dreamed he would one day stand next to the president of the United States. Born to poor migrant workers, Gonzales grew up in a two-bedroom house shared by his family of ten. There was no telephone or hot water. Because his parents were too poor to send him to college, Gonzales joined the Air Force, but after two years obtained an appointment to the Air Force Academy and, from there, transferred to Rice University. College was still a time of struggle for Gonzales, who had to sell refreshments in the bleachers during football games to support himself. But he eventually went on to Harvard Law School and rose to prominence in the Texas government. And then one day, decades after rising from his humble beginnings in Texas, he found himself standing next to President George W. Bush at the White House. The president had nominated him to be the nation's first Hispanic attorney general. As he accepted the nomination, Gonzales embraced the president and said, "'Just give me a chance to prove myself'—that is a common prayer for those in my community. Mr. President, thank you for that chance."

Like Gonzales, many Hispanics in America and elsewhere have shed humble beginnings to soar to impressive and previously unreachable heights. In the twenty-first century, influential Hispanic figures can be found worldwide and in all fields of endeavor including science, politics, education, the arts, sports, religion, and literature. Some accomplishments, like those of musician Carlos Santana or author Alisa Valdes-Rodriguez, have added a much-needed Hispanic voice to the artistic landscape. Others, such as revolutionary Che Guevara or labor leader Dolores Huerta, have spawned international social movements that have enriched the rights of all peoples.

But who exactly is Hispanic? When studying influential Hispanics, it is important to understand what the term actually means. Unlike strictly racial categories like "black" or "Asian," the term "Hispanic" joins a huge swath of people from different countries, religions, and races. The category was first used by the U.S. census bureau in 1980 and is used to refer to Spanish-speaking people of any race. Officially, it denotes a person whose ancestry either descends in whole or in part from the people of Spain or from the various peoples of Spanish-speaking Latin America. Often the term "Hispanic" is used synonymously with the term "Latino," but the two actually have slightly different meanings. "Latino" refers only to people from the countries of Latin America, such as Argentina, Brazil, and Venezuela, whether they speak Spanish or Portuguese. Meanwhile, Hispanic refers only to Spanish-speaking peoples but from any Spanish-speaking country, such as Spain, Puerto Rico, or Mexico.

In America, Hispanics are reaching new heights of cultural influence, buying power, and political clout. More than 35 million people identified themselves as Hispanic on the 2000 U.S. census, and there were estimated to be more than 41 million Hispanics in America as of 2006. In the twenty-first century people of Hispanic origin have officially become the nation's largest ethnic minority, outnumbering both blacks and Asians. Hispanics constitute about 13 percent of the nation's total population, and by 2050 their numbers are expected to rise to 102.6 million, at which point they would account for 24 percent of the total population. With growing numbers and expanding influence, Hispanic leaders, artists, politicians, and scientists in America and in other countries are commanding attention like never before.

These unique and fascinating stories are the subjects of *The Twentieth Century's Most Influential Hispanics* collection from Lucent Books. Each volume in the series critically examines the challenges, accomplishments, and legacy of influential Hispanic figures, many of whom, like Alberto Gonzales, sprang from modest beginnings to achieve groundbreaking goals. *The Twentieth Century's Most Influential Hispanics* offers vivid narrative, fully documented primary and secondary source quotes, a bibliography, thorough index, and mix of color and black and white photographs which enhance each volume and provide excellent starting points for research and discussion.

# "There Were No Female Astronauts"

The day was June 18, 1983, and graduate researcher Ellen Ochoa, who normally spent her days at Stanford University in California immersed in the study of optical systems—the use of technology to give machinery the ability to "see"—was having trouble concentrating. Events were transpiring in Florida that day that would have significant effects on Ochoa's career plans. Ochoa had never considered working in the male-dominated field of space exploration. Today, though, for the first time an American woman was heading into space.

The excitement at Kennedy Space Center, Florida, that day was nothing unusual to the veteran astronauts and other members of the National Aeronautics and Space Administration (NASA) team. They had witnessed numerous launches before—of a space shuttle taking a crew into orbit around Earth and back. Those who had been at NASA the longest had watched rockets bearing crews and landing craft destined for the Moon.

This mission—Space Transportation System, Flight 7 (STS-7)—held a significance beyond the objectives of the many scientific experiments to be conducted. Among the shuttle's crew of five was Sally Ride, like Ochoa a graduate of Stanford University. Along with her four fellow astronauts, Ride waited for the moment when the rocket engines would ignite and the shuttle would lift off from its launching pad. When that moment arrived, Ride would become the first American woman to travel in space.

Until that moment, every achievement in America's space program had been attributed to the efforts of men. These included Alan B. Shepard Jr.'s inaugural fifteen-minute suborbital flight on May 5, 1961; John H. Glenn Jr.'s orbital flight on February 20, 1962; and the most renowned—Neil Armstrong and Edwin "Buzz" Aldrin Jr.'s descent to the Moon on July 20, 1969. Even the occasional space disasters, such as the death of three astronauts in a 1967 fire during a launch-pad test and the explosion aboard *Apollo 13* on the way to the Moon, involved male astronauts.

*Sally Ride, who in June 1983 became the first American woman in space, sleeps aboard the space shuttle.*

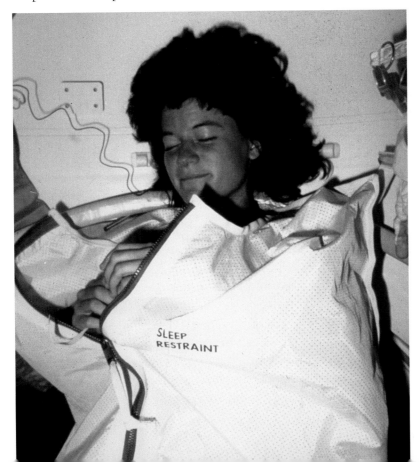

*Inspired by Sally Ride, Ellen Ochoa (shown here in training) pursued a career in the U.S. space program.*

For all the strides women had made in entering male-dominated professions during the previous decades, Ride's flight opened a new door. Before the mid-1980s Ochoa, a bright Californian, had barely given space exploration a thought as a career. No women had flown in space, so why, she reasoned, bother to pursue what appeared to be an unpromising path? As she told *Science Teacher* in 2005, "Having grown up during the Apollo era, I avidly followed flights to the Moon along with everyone else. However, women weren't accepted into the astronaut corps until I was halfway through college, so I hadn't considered it as a career when I was young."[1]

The tantalizing possibilities represented by Ride's historic flight prodded Ochoa into action. She entered the space program, a decision that would lead her to participate in four space shuttle missions. Even to this day, as prospects for additional assignments aboard the shuttle fade, Ochoa remains active as a NASA employee.

Ochoa's achievement adds another element to that of Ride's. While Ride's feats challenged other young women to pursue their dreams, Ochoa, whose paternal grandparents are Mexican, has broadened that challenge to include Hispanics. As part of the fastest-growing minority group in the United States, Ochoa feels that her occupation places her in the public eye more than most other jobs could and that what she does and says has an impact on thousands of other Hispanic women.

Ochoa's advice is to be persistent in pursuing the best education possible. "Don't be afraid to reach for the stars," she explains. "I believe a good education can take you anywhere on Earth and beyond."[2]

When her duties with NASA allow, Ochoa spends her days trying to inspire young people through speeches at high schools and colleges and through magazine articles encouraging them to strive to fulfill their dreams. She does not limit her appeals to people of Hispanic background, but she takes pride in her heritage and is pleased to be a role model for other Hispanic Americans.

Ochoa has succeeded admirably, both in her professional role as an astronaut and as an educator for the nation's youth. Yet she realizes that her success results from more than her personal effort. Her achievements, like those of many successful people, are in part attributable to a close, supportive family.

# Chapter 1

# "Education Can Open Doors"

In many ways, Ochoa experienced the same kind of challenges that many young Americans born in the latter half of the twentieth century faced. She endured a combination of hardships and obstacles that were tempered by love and guidance from a solid role model. At the same time, events rocked the United States and the world, ushering in the space age in which Ochoa was destined to play such a prominent part.

## Hispanic Heritage

Ellen Ochoa's birth very nearly coincided with the dawn of the space age. On October 4, 1957, seven months before Ellen was born, the nation that was known as the Soviet Union startled the world by successfully launching into orbit around Earth the basketball-size *Sputnik I*, the first artificial satellite. Though the small apparatus, which weighed less than 200 pounds (90.7kg), remained in space only a brief time, *Sputnik's* launch sent shock waves throughout the United States, which had long considered itself the technological leader in the world. It was therefore a radically changed world into which Ellen was born on May 10, 1958.

Soon the Ochoa family's circumstances changed as well. When she was one year old, the family moved from Los Angeles, California, to La Mesa, a suburb of San Diego. The family soon settled into the community, so much so that nearly four decades later Ochoa would still consider it her hometown.

Little Ellen was the third of five children, which included an older sister, Beth, and three brothers—older brother Monte and younger brothers Tyler and Wilson. The Ochoas had Hispanic roots. While both of Ellen's parents were born in the United States—Joseph in California and Rosanne in Oklahoma—Joseph's parents had migrated to the United States from the Mexican state of Sonora before he was born.

*The Soviet-made* Sputnik I *went into space in 1957 and was displayed at the World's Fair in Belgium the following year.*

Joseph had grown up speaking both Spanish and English, but in raising his own children, he preferred to downplay his Hispanic heritage. Discrimination against minority groups, such as Hispanic Americans, was common in the 1950s and 1960s, and Joseph believed his family would enjoy a better life by adopting Anglo (non-Hispanic) ways rather than clinging to Mexican traditions. While this decision was aimed at helping the Ochoa children avoid

# How to Be an Astronaut: Follow Your Dream

Daniel Barry, who flew with Ochoa in the 1999 STS-96 mission, seemed to know as a youth what he wanted to do with his life. The answer he gave during a NASA interview contains helpful advice for every young person—have a dream and follow through on it.

It's something that I dreamed about for a long time. I wanted

*Daniel Barry knew from a young age that he wanted to be an astronaut.*

to do this job for as long as I can remember. Way back in first grade when Mercury shots were going up, that wasn't unusual. Every kid in first grade wanted to grow up to be an astronaut. But as time went on different people wanted different goals, but this was one I had with me my whole life. And it's one thing to say it in first grade. It's a little different to say it in high school. It's substantially different to tell the chairman of your department while you're trying to get tenure that what you really want to do is go fly for NASA. So it's a dream I kept alive for a long time and I still pinch myself when I think about the opportunity I have to go fly.

Quoted in NASA, "Preflight Interview with Daniel Barry," STS-96. http://spaceflight. nasa.gov/shuttle/archives/sts-96/crew/int barry.html.

some discrimination at the hands of Anglos, it also cost the family some familiarity with its heritage, something Ellen later regretted.

> My Hispanic roots come from my father's side. His parents were Mexican, but my father was born in this country. He was one of twelve children. My father grew up speaking both Spanish and English but unfortunately he didn't speak Spanish with us at home. When I was growing up, my father believed as many people did at the time that there was a prejudice against people speaking their native language. It's really too bad, and I'm glad that things have changed in recent years.[3]

# A Mother's Influence

While her father seemed content, Ellen's mother never shied from asserting that she and her children could improve their situation, mainly by obtaining a quality education and working hard. Early on she became Ellen's role model, not only by what she said, but more particularly by what she accomplished, for Rosanne believed that a parent more effectively leads through actions than by words. "We all learned that a good education is about commitment and that education can open doors,"[4] Ellen once explained.

In addition to holding a full-time job and raising five children, Rosanne enrolled in classes at San Diego State University (SDSU). Since she could not abandon her family responsibilities and concentrate full-time on her education, Rosanne sought her college degree by taking one class a semester, usually at night, after laboring through a long day.

Rosanne's interests were wide-ranging, a fact that was not lost on Ellen. "She was going to college the whole time I was growing up," she later recalled. "She studied whatever interested her—business, biology, journalism, linguistics—she just finds all kinds of subjects very interesting. She was always talking about her classes."[5]

Ellen admits that she looked to her mother as the prime role model in her life. She especially noticed how her mother never gave up, despite the rigors of tending to her family while attempting to squeeze in rigorous college courses. Rosanne's efforts to set an example of steadfast determination would pay off. After twenty years of studying, and two years after her daughter, Ellen, received her college degree, Rosanne would earn a liberal arts degree from SDSU. In the process, Ellen and her siblings learned the value of persistence and the importance of an education. Possibly as a consequence of their mother's example, all five of the Ochoa children would complete college degrees.

Ellen makes no secret of who she credits with her own success. "I had a number of teachers that certainly encouraged me in specific areas, or just overall were important influences," she said in a preflight interview with NASA in 2002, "but I think the number one influence would be my mother partly just because of the way she raised me and my four siblings, and partly because of her love of learning. She went to college part-time for twenty years, and finally graduated a couple of years after I did."[6]

## "I Never Thought It Was a Career I Could Grow Up and Pursue"

One reason Rosanne had to do so much on her own was that she and Joseph divorced when Ellen was in junior high school. The months following the divorce were difficult for Ellen and the other Ochoa children, but Rosanne would not allow them to use the emotionally charged situation as an excuse for not doing what they were supposed to do. She insisted they apply themselves at school, set goals, and work hard to achieve them.

Despite the divorce and her longing for her absent father, Ellen studiously applied herself in every subject. She did well in any class she took, but she loved the orderliness and sense of structure that math and science seemed to offer. She played the flute for the school band and enjoyed reading science fiction. She especially loved Madeleine L'Engle's *A Wrinkle in Time*, the tale of three children who travel through space and time. At age thirteen Ellen won the San Diego school spelling bee, and she was named the outstanding student in junior high school.

Despite her obvious talent for math and science, thirteen-year-old Ellen had no idea what she wanted to do as an adult. Two years earlier, in 1969, the eleven-year-old had watched in fascination the television images of Armstrong taking the historic first

*Neil Armstrong, commander of the 1969 Apollo 11 space mission, takes the first human steps on the moon.*

steps on the Moon. Still, Ochoa recalls that the event had not sparked a sudden interest in traveling to the heavens, since up to that point women had played no publicly prominent role in the nation's space program. "At that time women were excluded from becoming astronauts, so I never thought it was a career I could grow up and pursue."[7]

In the late 1960s, women were just beginning to assert their rights and demand a role equal to that of men in American society. For as long as anyone could remember, a woman's place had been rigidly defined as caring for the home and children, with little expectation of stepping into other careers long open to men. Although prospects for women were changing, in 1969 the thought of a woman joining Armstrong and other astronauts in space was not in the picture.

## Positive Examples

Certain educators reinforced the notion that a woman could not be an astronaut. When Ochoa attended Grossmont High School in La

# The *Challenger* Disaster

Disasters anywhere in the world gain people's attention and sympathy, but when they occur in a field in which a person hopes to excel, the tragedy tales on greater significance. In a 2006 interview, Ellen Ochoa describes her reaction to the loss of the *Challenger* crew:

> Like everyone in the country, I was stunned by it. At the time, I was working at Sandia National Laboratories and didn't personally know anyone at NASA, but I had submitted an application to NASA and knew that it was being considered in the astronaut selection that was planned for that year. Even so, it didn't affect my desire to become an astronaut, and I continued to pursue that.

Written response to author's queries, May 26, 2006.

*The space shuttle* Challenger *exploded in 1986, killing all six astronauts on board.*

Mesa, her counselors discouraged her and other female students from taking math and science, subjects that many people viewed as male realms. Fortunately for Ellen, at the same time she also had teachers who by their example disproved such outmoded ideas and prodded her to pursue her ambitions. For example, her calculus teacher, Paz Jensen, refused to prejudge her students' potential. She also made the subject fun and tried to show how the subject related to her students' lives. Ochoa says that it was because of Jensen's influence that she started to consider mathematics as a possible major in college.

"My high school calculus teacher, Ms. Paz Jensen, made math interesting," Ochoa explained in an interview. "She encouraged her students to do well and to continue in math."[8] The strong role model that Jensen provided helped Ochoa see that not only could women be excellent instructors in a demanding field, but that she could pursue whatever subjects she found interesting.

Two other women, American literature teacher Jeanne Dorsey and British literature teacher Dani Barton, also made classes interesting and prodded Ellen to excel. For example, instead of assigning the class to read a poem or a short story and answer the textbook's questions, the pair challenged students to search major pieces of literature for meaningful themes and to look for how the messages conveyed by the authors could make an impact on people. They wanted Ellen and other students to see that school was not just a simple exercise in memorizing disconnected facts, but a necessary step in preparing for a career and developing one's intellect.

*Like the student shown here, Ochoa took advanced math classes in high school.*

"I was always drawn to teachers who made class interesting," said Ochoa. "In high school, I enjoyed my American and English literature classes because my teachers, Jeanne Dorsey and Dani Barton, created an environment where interaction was important."[9]

Ellen flourished under such influence, but she did not limit her excellence to the classroom. She had set her sights on attending college, and counselors made it clear that universities searched for well-rounded applicants. The better colleges preferred students who displayed a broad spectrum of interests, such as sports, community service, school clubs, student government, or music, rather than applicants who buried themselves in academics to the exclusion of everything else.

Ellen had long enjoyed music and had learned to play the flute earlier in her life. Her musical talent blossomed in high school, and she was good enough to be selected to play with the San Diego Civic Youth Orchestra. Audiences raved about her performances, and soon Ellen was known throughout the city for her musical talent.

*Ochoa poses with her fellow astronauts during a 1994 space mission.*

Despite a busy and diverse extracurricular life, Ellen graduated from Grossmont High School in 1975 as class valedictorian, meaning she had the highest grade point average in her class. As a result of her effort, a steady stream of offers from colleges and universities came her way. Prestigious Stanford University dangled a four-year scholarship in hopes of luring Ellen to its campus south of San Francisco, in Palo Alto, but she declined the offer. She wanted to remain near San Diego, where she would be close to her family and could help her mother raise the younger children.

# San Diego State University

Because she wanted to remain close to home, Ochoa enrolled at San Diego State University (SDSU). In the beginning she had no idea what she wanted to study in college. She first thought of pursuing engineering, but one of her professors advised her to explore other fields, saying that engineering was too hard for a woman. Ochoa discounted the advice, noting that there were few women working in the disciplines that most interested her. "I don't think I had a single woman science or engineering professor my entire ten years of college [including graduate school]," stated Ochoa later. "In many cases, I was the only female student in the class as well."[10]

Still, because she was unsure of what she wanted to study, Ochoa enrolled in a variety of courses, including music and business classes. In her first two years at SDSU, Ochoa changed her major five times, finally settling on physics, a field in which few women had gained prominence. As she explained to NASA in 2002, "I think my interest in math is probably what led me into science and engineering."[11]

Ochoa later recalled what ultimately led her to physics:

> I always liked math in school, and took calculus in high school and finished it up in college even though I wasn't, at that time, studying in math and science. And that's kind of what led me to look at the fields of study that used math and used calculus and differential equations and that's what got me interested in physics.[12]

As she had in high school, Ochoa excelled in her studies and graduated from SDSU as the class valedictorian in 1980. Armed

*Ochoa studied physics at San Diego State University. Pictured here are students on the university campus.*

with a bachelor's degree in physics, Ochoa now turned to the school that she had rebuffed only five years prior.

## Stanford University

Stanford had never lost interest in Ochoa, even though she had turned down their scholarship offer in 1975. When Ochoa graduated from SDSU with top honors, Stanford's engineering school, one of the most highly regarded in the nation, extended another offer that included financial aid. This time Ochoa accepted, since she would have the opportunity to spend years doing research and studying with top-notch educators. Knowing that her younger siblings were now older and better able to look after themselves helped her make the decision, since Ochoa knew her mother needed less help at home.

Ochoa focused on electrical engineering, the discipline that deals with how electricity can be applied to everyday use and is one of the most difficult subjects to master. Instead of seeing the difficulty of the subject as an obstacle, however, Ochoa relished the challenges it posed. She worked on a mathematical tool called

Fourier transforms, which are useful in the study of antennas, optics, and astronomy. Her professor was Joseph Goodman, long considered the top expert in optics and Fourier transforms and the author of an optics textbook used by most students.

With Goodman providing guidance, Ochoa immersed herself in research. Optics includes the study of light and how people see things. In the course of her work, Ochoa studied holograms, which are three dimensional images, and the lasers used to create them. The research had practical applications. For instance, Ochoa worked with computers that produce images a doctor might use in diagnosing an illness or determining the course of treatment for a patient.

## Courage to Succeed

She is a role model for all to try their best in everything they do. Ellen is a scientist, inventor, astronaut, classical flutist, wife, and mother of two little boys. Clearly these descriptors are not in order of importance, but all demonstrate her courage to succeed.

Molly Murphy MacGregor, "Celebrating Women of Courage and Vision," National Women's History Project. www.feminist.com/resources/artspeech/genwom/celebrate.htm.

The work did not always come easy to Ochoa. The research called for long hours and weeks of studying complicated ideas and procedures. However, she was comforted knowing that she was not the only person going through difficult times.

> There were times when as a Ph.D. student, I sometimes felt like quitting. In doing research, sometimes you hit a dead end, or are getting results in the lab that you just don't understand, and it's not clear how to proceed. What helped me was to find out that other students went through the same thing, and even my professors talked about the problems they had as students. One of them told me that receiving a Ph.D. not only meant that a person had contributed new knowledge in a specific field, but that the person had shown great persistence and overcome obstacles and uncertainty.[13]

## Chapter 2

# "Being Prepared for a Great Adventure"

The path leading to a career as an astronaut had actually begun while Ochoa was still in graduate school. One day a colleague of Ochoa's mentioned that he had applied for a position as an astronaut and suggested that Ochoa do the same. She had never before considered space exploration as a vocation, but her associate's comments prodded her to check into how one became an astronaut. That decision turned out to be a momentous one.

## To NASA

Ochoa's investigation of opportunities for women at NASA revealed some intriguing facts. As she learned more about the agency, she realized that NASA offered prominent roles to women, not only on the ground but in the astronaut corps itself. Suddenly the notion of becoming an astronaut did not seem so far-fetched.

> When I was in graduate school, some friends of mine were applying to the astronaut program, so that's when I decided to find out more about the program, and I

became real excited about doing it, once I realized that I would be eligible to apply. And it just seemed like such a great way to combine my interest in research and engineering as well as space exploration.[15]

Ochoa approached the task of gaining entrance to the astronaut corps with typical intensity and drive. To Ochoa it was as if she had suddenly spotted an immense treasure that had been just hidden from view. She later recalled:

The 1978 group of astronauts, the first astronauts picked for the shuttle, was very significant because of the variety of backgrounds of the selectees, including all kinds of science and engineering fields, and because it included the first six women ever chosen to be U.S. astronauts.

*The first six American women astronauts were (left to right) Rhea Seddon, Anna Fisher, Judith Resnick, Shannon Lucid, Sally Ride, and Kathryn Sullivan.*

At the time, I had never considered being an astronaut, but a few years later, when I was a graduate student at Stanford and realized I might be in a position to apply, I was encouraged by the fact that women were doing this job and that Sally had been a student at Stanford, just like I was.[16]

Now, only a handful of years after NASA selected that initial group of women astronauts, Ochoa decided to try to join that select group, despite a grueling application process. In 1985 she applied for the first time. This involved composing pages of typewritten responses to numerous questions, sitting through lengthy interviews, and going through in-depth physical examinations. Although NASA turned her down, Ochoa quickly reapplied the next year and each year after, despite the time demanded by the application process, which had to be started from scratch each time.

Ochoa's persistence was a product of her upbringing. Her mother had emphasized that one succeeds through a combination of education and hard work. Ochoa already possessed the education, and she now hoped that the hard work she was putting forth would make the difference.

## Persistence Pays Off

Ochoa set out to make herself a more attractive candidate in NASA's eyes. She took flying lessons and obtained a private pilot's license. She continued to make time for outside interests, such as her flute playing, to show that she was a well-rounded individual rather than just a scientist concerned only with laboratory research.

Because she believed she had the necessary qualities to be an astronaut, Ochoa persisted. Despite being turned away by NASA, she felt that she could one day convince the agency of that fact. "That's very important—not giving up," Ochoa explained later. "It [being an astronaut] definitely is one of those jobs where you can increase your skills and career achievements, and continue to reapply."[17]

Ochoa also came to understand that she faced an obstacle the other candidates did not face. Whereas others had been planning a career as an astronaut for years, she had arrived at the decision only recently. She had much ground to make up. In an interview for the Smithsonian Institute she said,

> A lot of my friends in the astronaut program decided when they were very young that when they grew up that they wanted to become an astronaut. They decided from a very young age, maybe even younger than you [the Smithsonian's interviewer], that that's what they would do; they would go to college and study engineering, and try to join the program.

> But for me, it was a little different. For one thing, when I was your age, we had astronauts who landed on the moon for the first time—probably when I was about your age, about eleven. But at that time, there weren't any women astronauts and also very few who were scientists. Most of them were pilots in the military at that point. So it didn't occur to me when I was in school that this was something I could grow up and do. But

# Rejection

Some people may think that the road to NASA was easy for Ellen Ochoa. Like most success stories, however, she encountered many obstacles along the way. Also in a way similar to other success stories, she found a way to either overcome those obstacles or use them in her behalf. In a 2006 interview, she explained how she handled her initial rejections from NASA.

In 1987, when only thirteen people were chosen from thousands of applicants, I wouldn't say that I felt rejected. I was actually quite thrilled and surprised to make it to the group of one hundred that were interviewed, and to find out I had scored well. It motivated me to continue to pursue the astronaut career. I decided to get a pilot's license, which I did a year later, and also decided I wanted to work for NASA so that I could be involved in space exploration in my research work.

Written response to author's queries, May 26, 2006.

as the space program evolved as I said we've moved more from piloting into science and engineering.[18]

Ochoa's effort slowly paid off. In 1987 she was among one hundred finalists for twenty-some positions, and although she once again fell short, this was closer than she had ever come before. Finally, in January 1990 NASA announced that Ochoa had been selected as one of the twenty-three persons who would train to be astronauts that year. Ochoa was now poised to be the first Hispanic woman in America's astronaut corps.

*Ochoa trains with a parachute at Vance Air Force Base in Houston, Texas.*

Ochoa is proud of her Hispanic heritage, but she does not believe that it played any role in being selected by NASA. "Getting to be an astronaut is tough for anybody, not just Hispanics or women. I don't think my background made it harder or easier. I think it's just a matter of working hard to have a very good education."[19]

# Training for the Skies

Being selected for the astronaut corps was only the beginning. Ochoa had to complete the arduous training program at Johnson Space Center in Houston, Texas. The candidates were required to master diverse and difficult subjects such as oceanography and orbital mechanics. In addition Ochoa and her fellow trainees had to master land and water survival techniques. As with every other challenge in her life, Ochoa dealt with every obstacle in turn. By July 1991 she had passed every class and could turn to the more exciting work of preparing for an actual space shuttle mission.

Shuttle astronauts are placed in two categories—those that fly the spacecraft (pilots), and those who execute the shuttle's many experiments and other assignments (mission specialists or payload specialists), such as deploying satellites. For the next two years, Ochoa trained

# Training

As often as Ellen Ochoa would love to head into space, most of her time with NASA is spent on the ground, either training for another mission or doing other kinds of work. Instead of seeing her ground work as limiting, Ochoa loves the variety offered it provides. She explained this in a 2005 interview with *Science Teacher:*

> One aspect of my job that I really enjoy is the variety. When I'm training for a flight, I spend a lot of time in simulators planning, rehearsing, and problem-solving for all phases of a mission. For example, we use a motion-based simulator to practice launches and landings, robotic simulators (both computer-based and hardware-based, including one underwater) to practice the tasks involving robot arms, and experimental hardware or software to learn about scientific procedures. One day I could fly in a high-performance jet to Florida to train with some hardware there and gain crew coordination experience. Another day I could scuba dive in our big training pool to learn about the tasks being performed by the spacewalking crewmembers on my flight.

Quoted in Megan Sullivan, "An Interview with NASA Astronaut Ellen Ochoa," *Science Teacher*, February 2005, p. 2.

*Astronauts prepare for space travel by training in a zero-gravity environment.*

for her mission, scheduled to launch in April 1993. She spent most of the time on the ground, working with other crew members or studying the intricacies of her assigned mission duties, while also completing other NASA requirements, such as public appearances or writing reports on the progress of the mission's preparations.

Ochoa soon learned that even though astronauts are assigned to specific shuttle missions, crew members often do not train together. In a given week, the shuttle pilots might be in one location, practicing takeoffs and landings in simulators, while Ochoa and other mission specialists might be elsewhere learning how to conduct one of the planned experiments, since these are not necessarily directly related to their own academic field.

One of the distinctive features of training for a shuttle mission is that Ochoa and the other astronauts not only spent hundreds of hours learning their own duties, but they also learned how to perform the duties of fellow astronauts. This cross-training ensured that in an emergency, when one astronaut may be disabled, another could step in and complete the assignment. NASA demands that their astronauts possess numerous skills, but few are as important as teamwork. The astronauts need to know that not only is every person aboard the shuttle thinking about the mission's overall goals instead of his or her own objectives, but that someone can back up each astronaut in critical duties.

"An astronaut needs to be able to put the team's goals above personal goals," explained Ochoa in 2006. "He or she must be able to work compatibly with and gain the respect of the other team members, and must be able to motivate the team to accomplish goals and tasks."[20]

## Simulated Experiences

Besides building a sense of teamwork, Ochoa and the other astronauts scheduled for the 1993 mission spent days and weeks on dozens of simulators—machines designed to re-create as closely as possible the conditions they would face during the mission, from the extreme gravitational forces created on blastoff to the sensation of weightlessness in orbit. Ochoa did not simply experience a simulated takeoff a single time—she and her crewmates went through the simulation numerous times. In that way, NASA hoped to see to it that the astronauts would be prepared for whatever situations might arise.

Various machines helped the astronauts prepare. In the motion base simulator, for instance, a strapped-in Ochoa was spun in several different axes to produce the feel of launching and reentry, while the centrifuge whipped her in circles faster and faster to give her the crushing, almost violent sensation she would experience during launch. When Ochoa needed to

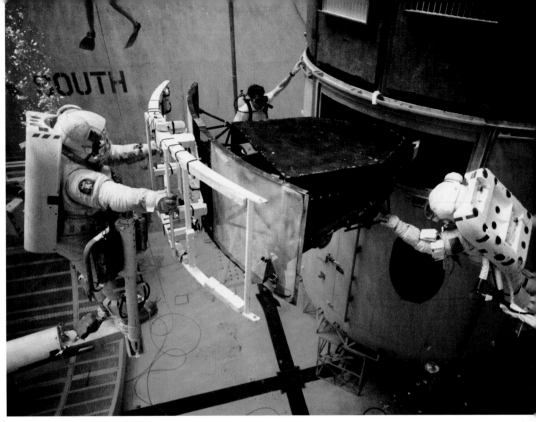

*Training underwater helps astronauts get ready for the weightlessness they will experience in space.*

practice the work she would perform once in orbit, she stepped into the fixed base simulator, a duplicate of the shuttle's flight deck. Ochoa also trained with the engineering simulator, an elaborate piece of equipment that replicated as closely as possible the conditions she would encounter in orbit, to practice space rendezvous.

Ochoa quickly learned that NASA not only wants astronauts to be prepared to do what is expected, but they should be ready to face the unexpected as well. Emergencies frequently arise during space missions, and the people who fly the shuttle need to know how to handle various crises. Consequently, during training NASA often tosses problems at the astronauts for them to solve. Ochoa might be using the motion base simulator, going through her duties, when an alarm indicates that a malfunction has occurred. In only a few minutes' time, she must arrive at a solution and begin to carry out the required steps.

"To be a good astronaut, the person must have a sense of judgment," explained Ochoa in 2006. "NASA wants us to use the information we have at hand, know what resources are available with which to solve the problem, and then identify a logical, effective course of action."[21] The repeated practices help develop the ability to think quickly and logically under pressure.

For Ochoa, one of the most interesting simulators was the KC-135, a jet aircraft that makes the most ferocious roller-coaster ride pale in comparison. Once the plane gains sufficient altitude, the jet dips into such a steep descent that, for a period of twenty to thirty seconds, the occupants experience a feeling of weightlessness similar to what they experience in orbit. The aircraft, humorously dubbed the "Vomit Comet" by astronauts in recognition of the reaction the jet's motions often produce, continues flying up and down in broad arcs to give repeated periods of weightlessness. Other times, Ochoa and the other astronauts in training donned scuba gear and entered the Weightless Environment Training Facility, a large tank filled with water. Being buoyed by the water also lent a feeling of weightlessness.

These simulators helped prepare Ochoa for what she would experience in space. Though they assisted to a large degree, Ochoa realized that the simulators could only reproduce a small portion of what she would feel. Only the launch and the mission in orbit itself could provide her with a true understanding.

## "I Never Felt Like Quitting"

One drill, in particular, brought home to Ochoa how perilous a space journey can be. The crew often had to practice what to do in case of an abort—the ending of the mission during the critical seconds during blastoff—due to a serious malfunction. The simulator would hurl different abort scenarios at the astronauts, and if they reacted correctly, they would be rated as having survived. If they reacted incorrectly, they would be declared dead. Such simulator "deaths" are part of the astronauts' routine. Astronaut Brewster Shaw, the shuttle's pilot for the November 1983 STS-9 flight, recalled that he often had to go home to his family and tell them that he and the crew had again died in the simulator.

In addition to the many simulations, Ochoa had to master a range of subjects that outstripped anything a college student faced. Ochoa practiced scuba diving, sea and land survival tactics, piloting jet aircraft, and walking and working in a space suit. Among the many subjects she studied were geology, navigation, and astronomy. She also worked with virtual reality equipment that replicated the equipment she would use aboard the shuttle, thus helping her learn how to operate it proficiently in space.

## An Inspiration

Ellen's pioneering at NASA serves as an inspiration for young women with dreams of exploring outer space.

Womenworking.com, "Star-Trekking: Ellen Ochoa." www.womenworking2000.com/feature/index.php?id=81.

Ochoa recalls that her training was actually harder than the mission itself. As she noted in an interview in 2006, "Probably the hardest part of training is the amount and range of material that each astronaut is expected to learn and be able to apply. So it requires extra study and review time, good organizational skills, quick thinking, and the ability to ask good questions."[22]

Ochoa mentioned that despite the rigors, she never felt like giving up:

> I never felt like quitting because I could see I was learning a great deal, gaining skills, and, with the help of many trainers, being prepared for a great adventure that I very much wanted to take part in. Everyone on the ground team is willing to help out to get the astronauts prepared, to dig into technical issues, schedule specialized training sessions, etc.[23]

## To Launch Date

As the date for the launch neared, the training schedule intensified. Up to this point, Ochoa had generally spent part of each day preparing for her specific mission and the rest on the main desk job she held for NASA, which often consisted of public relations work. Nine months before the launch, however, her mission began absorbing more and more of her time, as much as ten hours a day. Sometimes her schedule was so full that she found little time for family, exercise, or relaxation.

*Ochoa poses with a model of the space shuttle.*

That family now included Coe Fulmer Miles, a fellow researcher Ochoa had met while at NASA's Ames Research Center. The two scientists both loved their research and shared a passion for volleyball, music, movies, and travel. They had married in 1990 and now, three years later, had to deal with the demand Ochoa's training placed on their spare time.

From six months to three months before launch, her schedule spilled into the weekends. After the three-month mark, desk work was abandoned altogether and replaced by more work in simulators and classes. Ochoa had to put on hold any correspondence until the late night hours, when she wearily headed home.

The final weeks before launch eliminated whatever free time Ochoa had previously enjoyed, as last-minute refinements in the mission's objectives and meetings occupied her entire waking time. The crew also conducted a full dress rehearsal for the countdown to launch.

This period was sometimes so exhausting and stressful that Ochoa and her fellow astronauts looked forward to the final days before the launch, when NASA would place them in quarantine. From that point on, except for a final brief reunion, Ochoa and her crewmates would not have any contact with family members. This was done to reduce the risk of bacterial or viral infection, since even something like a cold transmitted by a family member could lead to serious complications in orbit, where there was no doctor. During this period Ochoa wrote final notes to loved ones and made sure her will was in order. She did this just in case some catastrophic mishap should lead to her death. She also enjoyed a brief visit with family who traveled to the Kennedy Space Center. The bittersweet meeting was made awkward by the fact that Ochoa and the other astronauts could not move within touching distance of their loved ones.

Another step that emphasized the immensity of her undertaking was the requirement that Ochoa select two casualty-assistance officers. These were two astronauts not assigned to the mission whose duty was to care for her family while she was in orbit. These two astronauts' duties included handling the funeral arrangements should a deadly accident occur.

With the preparations and training complete, Ochoa turned her focus to the launch for her first mission. It was an event she would never forget.

# Chapter 3

# "What Engineer Wouldn't Want Those Experiences?"

Ochoa felt the excitement mount as the April 6, 1993, launching date neared. During training she had gained a sense of what space travel would be like, but Ochoa knew that only by experiencing an actual launch and mission could she truly understand the amazing sensations and emotions that every astronaut preceding her had gone through.

## The First Launch

On April 6 Ochoa joined commander Kenneth D. Cameron, pilot Stephen S. Oswald, and fellow mission specialists C. Michael Foale and Kenneth D. Cockrell for the ride to the launching pad, where the shuttle *Discovery* awaited. Cameron, Oswald, and Foale had been in space before; Ochoa and Cockrell were the only two rookies scheduled to make the voyage. The nine-day mission aimed to deploy a satellite and to conduct a variety of medical experiments and studies of the impact of solar activity on Earth.

Ochoa's mission opened with a setback. During the countdown, instrumentation monitoring the main propulsion system indicated that one of the valves meant to allow liquid hydrogen into the main engine was stuck in the off position, rather than the required on position. During the resulting "hold" in the countdown, analysis of the problem showed that the valve actually had opened, and that a sensor had malfunctioned. Still, the launch had to be rescheduled because the delay meant that the launch window—the brief time during which conditions were right—had been missed. Another attempt was set for April 8.

Ochoa gave little thought to the delay. She was disappointed that she had to wait two more days to reach space, but she did not worry more about her safety. "The delay was easily traced to a sensor problem," she later explained, "and the fix was straightforward, so I didn't have any special concern about it."[24]

On April 8 the rescheduled launch unfolded without a hitch. As expected for someone heading into space for the first time, a flood of emotions hit Ochoa, but she pushed them to the background because she had so many duties to perform. "Like most

*The space shuttle* Discovery, *with Ochoa aboard on her first mission, blasts off in April 1993.*

astronauts, I was very excited to get close to launch, after many years of dreaming about it. I was only concerned about two things: that I might get injured or sick and not be able to go, or that I might not do as good a job as I hoped and let people down. Fortunately, the mission went very successfully!"[25]

## Studying the Ozone Layer

After the giant rockets propelled *Discovery* into orbit around Earth, Ochoa and the crew quickly set about accomplishing the first of their objectives—the study of the ozone layer, a region of the atmosphere shielding Earth from the Sun's ultraviolet rays. The erosion of the ozone layer had concerned scientists and environ-

*Ochoa works aboard the space shuttle* Discovery.

*Launched by Ochoa from the space shuttle, the satellite* Spartan *flies through space.*

mentalists since the 1970s. A noticeable hole had developed over Antarctica, and subsequent measurements made by satellite indicated additional erosion elsewhere about the globe. Scientists feared that without the full protection provided by the ozone layer, the incidence of skin cancer among humans could rise precipitously. Also, food crops could be damaged due to an overabundance of sunlight and heat.

Ochoa and the other mission specialists, in conjunction with scientists on the ground from Germany, France, Belgium, the Netherlands, and Switzerland, were assigned to study this issue. Part of Ochoa's assignment was to deploy a satellite that would record observations and data on the velocity and acceleration of solar wind—the powerful winds and energy bursts that exist on the Sun—and its impact on the ozone layer. Ocho explained in 1999:

> On my first flight, we studied ozone depletion of the Earth's atmosphere. We measured a wide variety of chemicals in the air. Measuring the concentration at different altitudes and the amount of energy coming from

the sun were a way to understand important atmospheric chemical reactions. We took measurements during the entire mission which are put into a precise database and later used to correct and re-calibrate instruments and data on orbiting satellites.[26]

Ochoa was responsible for one of the most difficult duties of the mission—operating the Remote Manipulator System, or robotic arm, to cautiously move the satellite from the shuttle's cargo bay into space, then retrieve it two days later. The 2,800-pound satellite (1,270kg) would operate on its own as it gathered information about particles emitted by the Sun.

---

## A First

It was never Ellen Ochoa's childhood dream to become an astronaut, but her love of mathematics took her through postgraduate programs all the way to NASA and, in 1993, earned her a spot in the history books as the first Hispanic woman in space.

Guadalupe Bellavance, "Ellen Ochoa, First Hispanic Woman in Space," EFE World News Service, June 9, 2004. http://80-infotrac.galegroup.comepass.tin.lib.mi.us.

---

Using the robotic arm, Ochoa successfully nudged the satellite, called *Spartan*, from its rack in the cargo bay on April 11. The shuttle followed about 23 miles (37km) behind the satellite to avoid the possibility of a collision, then two days later moved closer so Ochoa could again maneuver the robotic arm to retrieve the satellite. Oswald manually flew *Discovery* the final few hundred feet (meters) to close on *Spartan*, when Ochoa carefully grabbed the mechanism with the robotic arm and returned it safely to its cargo-bay rack.

# SAREX II

Ochoa also played a crucial role in the other main objective—communicating with the Russian *Mir* space station and with students around the globe through the Shuttle Amateur Radio Experiment II (SAREX II). The contact with *Mir* proved to be the first time that communication had been made with the space station using ama-

# Determination

Rick Husband, who flew in space with Ellen Ochoa during the STS-96 mission, explained in an interview with NASA how he became an astronaut. His answer reveals the important role that determination plays in success.

From the time when I was four years old, when the Mercury Program first got started, I was in front of the TV for every one of the launches. And the whole time I was growing up, for as long as I can remember, anytime anybody asked me what I wanted to be, it was "I want to be an astronaut." And so I worked toward that goal for years and years and was fortunate enough to get selected.

Quoted in NASA, "Preflight Interview with Rick Husband," STS-96. http://spaceflight.nasa.gov/shuttle/archives/sts-96/crew/inthusband.html.

*Rick Husband (foreground) and Ilan Ramon prepare for a video tour aboard* Columbia. *Both astronauts and their fellow crew members later died when the shuttle disintegrated on landing.*

teur radio equipment. And in a separate activity, Ochoa chatted directly with students in different nations according to a preset schedule. Using the call sign KB5TZZ, Ochoa answered students' questions and helped promote interest in science and space among the world's youngsters. In doing this, NASA hoped to spark public interest in the shuttle program and to promote educational opportunities involving astronauts and students. As time permitted, Ochoa and some of the other crew members also established contact with amateur ham radio operators about the globe.

As an additional step in increasing student awareness of the shuttle program and for creating renewed interest among young-sters in science and technology, NASA developed a teachers' guide titled "Atmospheric Detectives." The lesson plans, targeted for middle schools, suggested ways that teachers could incorporate the activities of Ochoa and the crew of *Discovery* into their class-room. Different lessons combined mathematics, chemistry, physics, and Earth sciences with problem-solving activities.

## Other Experiments

Ochoa was involved in many other experiments besides the two main objectives of releasing and retrieving the satellite and estab-

*Ochoa poses with other crewmembers aboard the space shuttle* Discovery *in April 1993.*

lishing communications with students. She and the other two mission specialists also conducted a bone cell differentiation experiment. In this study, Ochoa, Foale, and Cockrell observed mouse bone cells to determine how well they grow in microgravity, the technical term for the effectively weightless conditions in Earth orbit. This study contributed information on possible treatments of bone diseases among humans and ways to prevent bone deterioration among the elderly on Earth as well as in astronauts during extended future missions.

In another experiment, the three mission specialists were required to hatch tiny shrimp eggs in space so they could study the effects of microgravity on the development of the newly hatched shrimp. This experiment's main purpose was to determine whether shrimp could be used as a food source during long space missions, such as an eventual trip to Mars for which NASA was planning.

Other experiments examined potential ways to harness plants to produce oxygen; looked at whether microgravity enhances the growth of cells that can be used to battle leukemia, lymphoma, and breast cancer; and investigated whether drugs to prevent breast cancer and AIDS could be developed.

# Return to Earth

Although NASA kept Ochoa and the crew busy most of the time, Ochoa found a few moments of leisure time in which she entertained everyone with her flute. After playing "The Marine Corps Hymn" for Cameron, she offered a few classical pieces by Vivaldi and Mozart. As she played, a weightless Ochoa drifted toward a shuttle window, where she had an amazing view of a brilliantly blue Earth. "It's a very fond memory," she said of the scene. "It was just very peaceful."[27]

One aspect of playing music in space that Ochoa enjoyed involved the sheet music. In the weightlessness of space, she needed no extra equipment to hold the paper. "You can hold the music up and you don't even need a music stand,"[28] she explained.

After a successful nine-day voyage, Ochoa and the crew of STS-56 prepared for their return to Earth. They secured equipment in storage lockers, then fired rockets designed to gradually slow the shuttle's speed and lower its orbit. On April 17, 1993, one day after NASA canceled a scheduled April 16 landing due to bad weather on the ground in Florida, *Discovery* touched down at Kennedy Space Center. Having experienced the wonders and beauty of space travel, Ochoa was eager for more. She did not have to wait long.

# STS-66

On Thursday, November 3, 1994, Ochoa headed into orbit for her second voyage, this time in the shuttle *Atlantis*. She and five other astronauts, including Jean-Francois Clervoy, a French astronaut from the European Space Agency, departed Kennedy Space Center for an eleven-day mission. Ochoa again studied the sun's energy, which can come in bursts, and the effects those bursts have on Earth's ozone layer. This time Ochoa focused on measuring the middle layer of the atmosphere above the northern hemisphere and on detecting any damage that had occurred from solar activity, as well as examining how the atmosphere changed as the winter season neared. As payload commander, Ochoa was in charge of the scientific studies carried out in orbit, and as she had in STS-56, she again used the shuttle's robotic space arm to deploy and retrieve a satellite.

Again, safety concerns caused a delay—although this time it was brief. Five minutes before launch, NASA officials delayed the countdown for three minutes and forty-three seconds, while managers consulted with meteorologists about potentially violent weather at some of the abort sites. Those locations, airstrips on islands in the Atlantic Ocean and in Africa, were places where the shuttle could safely return to Earth in an emergency, and NASA would not approve the launch until assured that acceptable weather existed at these sites. The last thing NASA's managers wanted to do was send six astronauts and the expensive shuttle into a severe storm, where lightning or unpredictable winds could cause an accident. The NASA officials determined that all was well, and shortly before noon on November 3, the rocket engines rumbled to life and lifted *Atlantis* into space.

# The Value of the Space Station

Every astronaut, including Ellen Ochoa, recognizes the important role the International Space Station plays for space exploration. They try to educate the world that, even though the station remains in orbit around Earth, it is the launching pad for expeditions into deep space. Astronaut Julie Payette, who accompanied Ochoa in the 1999 mission, explained the space station's importance in a preflight interview with NASA:

> The International Space Station is just a step in our normal progression as human beings. We have been pushing our frontiers all along. When our frontiers were one continent, then we explored further and found others. Our kind of frontier today is space, and when we think about it, we haven't been that far. We've been on Earth and we've been once or twice to the moon several decades ago. But we now know that we're part of a universe in which we are not even a grain of salt compared to the size and vastness of this universe. We haven't been to another planet inside our own solar system. Our frontiers have been right up there just outside the orbit of the Earth.

Quoted in NASA, "Preflight Interview with Julie Payette," STS-96. http://spaceflight.nasa.gov/shuttle/archives/sts-96/crew/intpayette.html.

## The Ozone Layer

On Friday, November 4, Ochoa used the robotic arm to gently lift the satellite from the payload bay and send it into its own orbit. As Ochoa explained to the Smithsonian Institution shortly after the mission, the robotic arm is extremely agile, thanks to its structure, which mimics a human limb.

> We have a fifty foot long arm that we can take up on the Shuttle and we used it to display and retrieve a science satellite. This arm is a lot like your own arm. It has a wrist joint. It has an elbow joint, and it has a

*Ochoa works alongside a fellow astronaut on* Atlantis *during the STS-66 mission in November 1994.*

shoulder joint. And we can operate it in a variety of ways. The most common way is that we have two hand controllers—kind of like a video game where we're trained to operate the arm to move all the joints at once so we can move from one position to any other position by moving these two hand controls. We can also operate it just joint by joint. So, if we want to move just the wrist joint or just the shoulder joint, we have a way of doing that.[29]

For the next eight days the satellite gathered information on the accumulation of gases in the middle and lower atmosphere above the northern hemisphere. In order to maintain a constant watch on the satellite and on other scientific experiments being simultaneously conducted, the six astronauts worked in two teams in twelve-hour shifts. Ochoa worked the Red Team, which in addition to herself included Donald McMonagle and Joseph Tanner. Meanwhile, Curtis Brown, Scott Parazynski, and Clervoy made up the Blue Team.

The satellite collected data that enabled scientists for the first time to construct three-dimensional maps of the middle atmosphere. By measuring gases that are distributed throughout the atmosphere by winds, scientists created a more accurate image than they had ever before had of conditions 10 to 30 miles (16 to 48km) above Earth. The satellite measured as many as forty different gases at the same time, and as Ochoa said in NASA's mission summary, the satellite was capable of detecting even the tiniest concentrations of gases, down to a few parts per billion. "Even though the quantities are small, these gases can play a large part in ozone destruction,"[30] she explained.

On November 9 Ochoa relayed details of a spectacular sight when she informed controllers on the ground that the crew could see as many as fourteen different layers in Earth's atmosphere as they observed the sunset. This observation and other knowledge gained during STS-66 helped scientists to more accurately understand the situation existing in the atmosphere.

On November 12, as *Atlantis* raced through the skies above New Zealand, Ochoa maneuvered the robotic arm to retrieve the satellite, which had completed its objective of gathering data for eight days. After inspecting the satellite while it was still connected to the arm, Ochoa then carefully returned the satellite to its spot in the payload bay. One successful experiment had ended, but others remained.

# Yielding Results

As was the case with the first shuttle mission she worked on, this one involved conducting many other scientific experiments besides the main one. These experiments kept Ochoa and her cohorts busy for much of the time—she and her Red Team astronauts enjoyed a half-day off on November 10—but NASA later concluded that they yielded results that have benefited society and also made the trip worthwhile.

On November 8, for example, Ochoa, McMonagle, and Tanner worked on a protein crystal growth experiment and a space tissue loss study to determine how microgravity in space affects the human body. The data from this study have been important for planning long-distance space flights, such as those to Mars and beyond, in which astronauts will be confined in spacecraft for months and even years. Scientists need to know how lengthy periods of weightlessness might affect vital body functions and muscular reaction.

Scientists also used information culled from color radar images taken of Earth to track ancient travel routes and to detect tiny movements of land located near volcanoes. Photos taken from the shuttle helped archaeologists map caravan routes that criss-crossed the Middle East in ancient times. The radar images clearly displayed lines—traces of paths etched in the ground by travelers hundreds of years ago—that were no longer visible to the unaided human eye. This information also enabled archaeologists to determine precisely the possible locations of ancient cities, since these would undoubtedly have been situated where the caravan lines intersected.

# Unexpected Information

Radar images taken from orbit also revealed other unexpected information. When the shuttle passed over the Sahara Desert in northern Africa, for instance, Ochoa could see the contours of land, but the radar images displayed an entirely different view. "It is just amazing," said astronaut Jeff Wilson, who flew two missions of his own in the shuttle. "You can see old rivers underneath the sand and things of that sort. It's like going on a treasure hunt."[31]

Another task involved using instruments to track from space slight land movements on Hawaiian volcanoes. Scientists hope to take this information and eventually use it to predict eruptions. This knowledge, scientists believe, could save many lives by giving those living near volcanoes time to evacuate in the event of an eruption.

The robotic arm was employed for more than the planned experiments, however. On November 12, Ochoa maneuvered the robotic arm to examine an icicle that had formed on the outside of the cargo-bay door during a normal water dump the day before. Television images captured by the robotic arm showed that the door's edges and latches were ice free and working properly, and following the directions of flight controllers, Ochoa used the robotic arm to break the icicle off the cargo bay's door.

*This satellite, launched as part of the STS-66 mission, gathered data about Earth's atmosphere.*

## Students and Space

At other times during the STS-66 mission, as she had on her previous flight, Ochoa turned to one of her most enjoyable duties—communicating with students on Earth. Ochoa says that during her time in space and while she is working on the ground, she most loves chatting with younger people and conveying positive messages about their futures and about what it takes to become an astronaut. She directs her comments to all students, but especially wants female students and those with a Hispanic American background to realize that nothing is beyond anyone who is intelligent and willing to work hard.

On November 4, while still in orbit, she answered high school honor students' questions about her job and her research during a television interview. She told the students that the aspects of space travel that gain the most attention from the public, such as the enormity of blastoff and sense of weightlessness, were certainly features she loved. "What engineer wouldn't want those

*Taken from the space shuttle* Atlantis, *this photograph shows remnants of long-ago volcanic activity in the Sahara Desert.*

experiences?" she asked. But she also tried to tell the students that being an astronaut was much more than a glorified thrill ride. "I always liked school, and being an astronaut allows you to learn continuously, like you do in school. One flight you're working on atmospheric research. The next, it's bone density studies or space station design."[32]

For Ochoa, the connection with students is more than simply a media link; she also feels a deep emotional bond to young people. For example, Ochoa carried with her into space the class ring belonging to Stacey Lynn Balascio, an aerospace engineering student at San Diego State University (SDSU) who had been hit and killed by a car only four days before she was due to graduate in May 1994. The student's death affected Ochoa because she and Balascio had similar backgrounds.

"It was my tribute to her," Ochoa explained. "Stacey was an Air Force ROTC (Reserve Officers' Training Corps) cadet. I'm a private pilot. Stacey was from my hometown, La Mesa,

California, and had graduated from Grossmont High School where I graduated from, too."[33]

The Society of Women Engineers at SDSU, an organization that Balascio had joined, planned a ceremony after Ochoa's shuttle mission during which Ochoa would return the ring to Balascio's parents. "She was very interested in flying," said Ochoa. "She wanted a career as an astronaut after completing her education. The Society celebrated her goals and accomplishments in engineering as a student member."[34] When Ochoa had completed her mission, she returned to SDSU for the ceremony, gave a speech honoring the girl, and then handed Balascio's ring to her proud parents.

## Mission Accomplished

On November 14, after completing 174 orbits, *Atlantis* returned to Earth. The landing was originally scheduled for Kennedy Space Center in Florida, but a combination of strong winds, rain, and clouds created by a tropical storm forced mission directors on the ground to divert the landing to Edwards Air Force Base in California.

NASA authorities were delighted at the work completed by Ochoa and the crew of *Atlantis*. Mission scientist Timothy Miller said, in evaluating the primary objective of the flight, that Ochoa and the other astronauts had performed "the most complete global health check on the atmosphere that has ever been done, measuring more trace gases that are important in ozone chemistry than any previous research effort."[35]

After analyzing the data and compiling a report on ozone variations in the atmosphere, scientists shared the results with the entire world. "The data belong to everybody," explained NASA Headquarters Program scientist Jack Kaye. "Following post-flight data analysis, the data ultimately will be deposited in Earth Observing System Data Information System archives at NASA's Goddard Space Flight Center, where it will be made available to atmospheric scientists from around the world."[36]

Ochoa had successfully completed two missions in two years. She experienced such amazing incidents and witnessed such astounding spectacles that she could hardly wait to once again return to space.

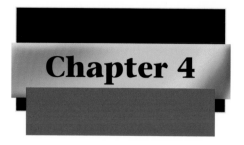

# Chapter 4

# "Going into Space Is Very Exciting"

That Ochoa was eager to participate in another mission was hardly surprising to those who know her. For someone with the deep-grained spirit of adventure that Ochoa possessed, no other place could match outer space. She loved every moment of her missions, from the grueling preparation and training, to the blastoff, and on to the excitement of the landing. For Ochoa, being an astronaut offers thrills and satisfaction she could obtain nowhere else.

## Before the Launch

Even though Ochoa finds satisfaction in the months of challenging training, for her the true excitement starts with launch day. Each mission commences with a multistep routine that begins with the crew gathering for the prelaunch breakfast. They then head to Kennedy Space Center where, with the help of assistants, they don 86 pounds (39kg) of gear, consisting of a space suit, two layers of long underwear, and survival equipment.

Now ready to enter the shuttle's cabin, Ochoa and the other astronauts climb into a vehicle called the Astrovan and ride to the waiting rocket, which towers above them. Water condensed from the humid air by the supercold propellant inside the fuel tank pours down from the shuttle in a constant waterfall.

The crew next rides an elevator 195 feet (59m) up to the platform outside the orbiter's hatch, where one by one they board the shuttle and are strapped into their seats—some in the cockpitlike flight deck and the others behind in the middeck—by another assistant, who connects four parachute clasps, four seat clasps, an oxygen line, and the headset. When Ochoa and the others feel the cooling effect of the water coming from a water line and circulating through the tiny tubes sewn into their long underwear, they know their mission is at hand. All they can do now is lie back and wait for the shuttle's engines to come alive and propel them into orbit.

The astronauts realize that the launch poses the riskiest part of their mission, but they control any fears or nervousness. They

*NASA's Astrovan (at right) transports astronauts to the launch pad at Kennedy Space Center.*

know that they have to put aside such distractions in order to focus on what lies ahead. Their bosses at NASA educate them about the risks, and everyone from Ochoa to the freshest recruit has the memory of the *Challenger*, which blew up seventy-three seconds after its launch on January 28, 1986, in their minds. The loss of those astronauts makes the dangers all too clear and forces them to realize that despite all the careful planning things can go wrong.

One of Ochoa's fellow astronauts, Franklin Chang-Diaz, says he had shoved the possibility of death to the background, but that *Challenger* shoved it immediately to the forefront. "I never, *ever* thought there was a tremendous danger, even though I knew intellectually there was," he said. After *Challenger*, "I realized I was vulnerable."[37]

To some, the safety record NASA had accumulated prior to *Challenger*'s loss was, given the uncertainties and risks of space travel, surprising. John Glenn, the first American to fly in orbit, admits that he thought many more deaths would occur as part of the space program.

Still, Ochoa claims not to be greatly worried. She states that the rewards outweigh the risks and that she rarely considers the perils of space travel. "I'm fortunate to carry out a very exciting, visible role," Ochoa stated in an interview, "which has included running experiments in space, operating robotic arms to deploy satellites, installing modules onto the International Space Station,

# Fun in Space

Though NASA keeps the astronauts busy in orbit, they manage to squeeze in some off time to relax, look out the window at Earth, or have fun. Ochoa played her flute on one flight.

Other astronauts used the 35-foot tunnel (10.7m) connecting the mid-deck to the laboratory module for an athletic competition. They stretched a huge rubber band normally used in exercising, called Dyna-Band, across the hatch. Each astronaut then shot themselves down the tunnel to see who went the farthest or who could make it all the way down the tunnel without touching the tunnel walls. Especially in space, where small mistakes can have devastating consequences, it helps to do something to relieve the tension.

and assisting the Commander and Pilot in launch, rendezvous, and landing procedure."[38] She adds that should anything occur, the astronauts have been carefully trained to deal with any problems that might arise.

# The Liftoff

Worries about something going wrong have to be put aside when a series of prelaunch events begin about two minutes before launch. The helmet visors come down, and oxygen courses through the line connected to the space suits. Ten seconds before launch the water deluge systems—a network of lines conducting water throughout the spacecraft—starts, creating a loud noise and sending vibrations through the shuttle. Four seconds later the main engine fires, adding to the noise and shaking.

That is nothing compared to the violence of the actual liftoff, when the shuttle roars into life with such force that the crew experiences the pressure against their bodies of 2g, double gravity. "The launch looks kind of slow to an observer," said astronaut Scott Kelly, "but when you're inside there ain't nothing slow about it. I mean, you feel all seven million pounds of that thrust. It's like this giant hand grabs the orbiter and throws it into space."[39] In the span of eight minutes, the shuttle zooms from a speed of 0 miles per hour (0kph) to an incredible 17,500 miles per hour (469kph).

"The vehicle explodes, literally explodes, off the pad," reported astronaut Mike McCulley, who noted that nothing in training quite prepares one for the real thing. "The simulator shakes you a little bit, but the actual liftoff shakes your entire body and soul."[40] Some compare the experience to being fastened to the front of a speeding freight train or being caught in an earthquake, while others claim they feel like an enormous bear is sitting on them. During one of Ochoa's missions, the crew noticed a layer of clouds 12,000 feet (3,658m) above them as they waited for ignition. They recalled that once the blastoff began, they were through that cloud layer before they could barely catch a glimpse of its approach.

Ochoa knows that on any shuttle flight the commander has abort options, meaning that if something goes wrong he or she can declare an emergency and order the mission abandoned. Those options vary, depending on when an emergency arises. The

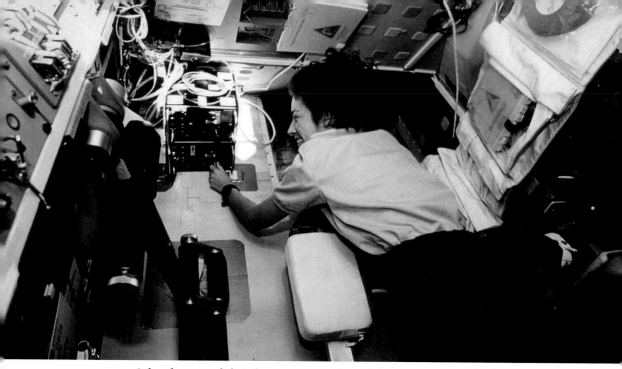

*Ochoa has stated that the experience of weightlessness is one of the things she loves most about space travel.*

commander can call for an abort-to-orbit, in which the shuttle attains a lower orbit than planned and then returns to Earth. Other choices are an abort-once-around, in which the shuttle circles Earth once at its intended altitude and returns; the transoceanic abort landing, in which the shuttle never gets to orbit but glides to a landing at a site in Europe or Africa; or the most risky, the return-to-launch-site, in which the shuttle's pilot attempts to return to Kennedy Space Center.

If all unfolds as planned during a launch, after a few minutes the shuttle reaches its planned altitude. At this point Ochoa and her crewmates hear a loud clang as the fuel tanks separate from the shuttle. They then hear the cannon-type eruptions as the pilot fires control jets to maneuver the shuttle into orbit.

## Weightlessness

Once in orbit, the astronauts grapple with weightlessness, which Ochoa has called one of the thrills of space travel. "It's hard to pick just one experience [as the best] because I've had so many amazing ones since joining the astronaut corps," Ochoa has said. "I vividly recall seeing Earth for the first time, trying to get used to moving around and working in zero gravity—it takes both less physical effort and more mental concentration than one might think—and the thrill of working with my crew to accomplish a difficult task."[41]

Due to weightlessness, the astronauts' bodily fluids shift around rather than remain evenly distributed. Their faces swell and become puffy. Because the fluid rushes to their heads, Ochoa and the other astronauts feel the same as if they were upside down on Earth, even though they are actually right-side up, a weird sensation that takes some adjustment. Still, astronaut Dave Williams asserts that if Disney created a ride with that same sensation, people would flock to it.

## Limitless Possibilities

How far do you want your education to take you? How about into outer space? If you think you can't make it that far, Dr. Ellen Ochoa will convince you that you can.

Anne Hart, "Without Limits," Graduating Engineer and Computer Careers Online. www.graduatingengineer.com/articles/minority/11-12-99.html.

Weightlessness affects the body in other, sometimes unpleasant ways. For example, freed of the pull of gravity, Ochoa's vertebrae moved slightly apart, a phenomenon that not only caused Ochoa to temporarily "grow" 1 to 2 inches (2.5 to 5cm), but placed extra strain on her lower back muscles. For any mission's first few days, Ochoa endured back pain.

Ochoa's legs also twitched in the first few days of weightlessness as her brain tried to figure out why gravity was no longer exerting its customary force on the body. This is a phenomenon that every astronaut experiences in space flights. "I noticed in the first four days of my flight that the muscles in my legs were twitching, firing all the time," said astronaut Rick Williams. "My brain wasn't getting any input from my muscles, and it was like saying, 'Hey, where's gravity?'"[42] To counter the effects of weightlessness, Ochoa spent time on the treadmill and other exercise equipment aboard the shuttle.

Ochoa and others also encounter space adaptation syndrome, or space sickness, caused when weightlessness affects the balancing organ known as the inner ear. More than half the astronauts become physically ill from the temporary condition, while the rest suffer from upset stomachs. Most feel fine by the third or fourth day, when they have had a chance to adjust to the unaccustomed conditions.

# Life Aboard the Shuttle

Once in orbit, the first thing Ochoa and the other members do is head to the middeck, remove the special garments worn for launch and entry, and put on their first set of clothes. Each astronaut brings a fresh outfit, provided by NASA, for each day in orbit, which he or she can then keep as souvenirs of the flight. The crew normally wear different colors, which correspond to rank. For instance, the commander might wear red, while a mission specialist like Ochoa might sport a blue outfit.

The astronauts do most of their work in an area about the size of an average living room. However, because in the weightless environment they can work on the "ceiling" as well as anywhere else in the quarters, the amount of usable space is much greater. A hatchway leads from the flight deck to the middeck, where the astronauts' sleeping quarters, storage lockers, toilet facilities, and the galley for cooking food are found.

NASA divides the working day into five-minute segments, with tasks assigned to each segment. That schedule has no slack built into it. If the crew fall behind in their jobs, the astronauts have to work into their designated sleeping time. Eight hours is set aside for sleeping, but beyond that little free time is available. During any breaks, Ochoa and her crewmates listen to music tapes, read books, look out at the amazing scenery that surrounds them, or watch movies.

One of the first adjustments Ochoa and her fellow astronauts must make is getting used to the routine sounds of the shuttle, for in the silence of space, small sounds that would go unnoticed on Earth are audible. For example, maneuvering the robotic arm to deploy or retrieve a satellite creates a noise that seems out of place in the quiet of space.

Ochoa was hardly alone in experiencing this feature—every astronaut goes through a similar occurrence. Astronaut Bob Cenker recalled his reaction when a satellite was deployed:

> I remember being warned about the sound the satellite
> makes as it leaves the cargo bay. The first time they did

# What a Golf Shot!

With the popularity of golf on the upswing, avid golfers everywhere would love to crash a golf ball as far as a Russian cosmonaut intends to do. Of course, the Russian will have a few advantages when he hits the ball—he will do so during a spacewalk outside the International Space Station. In the vacuum of space, the lucky Russian will propel the ball into orbit around Earth.

Russian space officials made an agreement with a Toronto, Canada, sporting goods company, Element 21 Golf Company, to use its equipment. A radio-transmitting golf ball will emit signals indicating its path. The Golf Shot in Space project will be done to honor the thirty-fifth anniversary of Alan Shepard's famous golf shot from the moon's surface

*Alan Shepard poses with a trophy he received for golf shots he made on the Moon during the Apollo 11 mission.*

one of these deploys, I'd been told that it scared everybody on board, because you mostly have silence in space. I mean, you hear fan noise, but people are attuned to the quiet. And when the satellite is deployed, you've got these explosive bolt cutters that release it. The shuttle is an all-metal structure, so the sound just rips through the vehicle.[43]

Ochoa, indeed every space traveler, had to get used to a host of minor differences between life on the ground and life aboard the shuttle. For example, every ninety minutes they experience a sunrise, as the shuttle completes one orbit of Earth in that amount of time.

Personal hygiene takes more effort in space than it does on the ground. In orbit, Ochoa uses a special rinseless soap and shampoo to clean herself in a sponge bath as no shower facilities are available in space. And when she brushes her teeth, she has to watch so that no toothpaste gets loose and floats throughout the shuttle's cabin.

The toilet accommodations are unlike anything on Earth. Rather than gravity to move along the waste, as on Earth, an airflow system is installed to move the waste to tanks aboard the shuttle, which are then cleaned out upon return to Earth. Ochoa states that while the bathrooms lack the comforts of those at home, she and the other astronauts quickly adapt.

## Food

The bathroom facilities are not the only inconvenient items aboard the shuttle. Ochoa and the others must subsist on freeze-dried meals,

*An astronaut rides the robotic arm of a space shuttle. Astronauts say the noise of the arm breaking the quiet of space can be startling.*

*Astronauts in orbit use a special rinseless shampoo to wash their hair.*

as it is too expensive to design a refrigeration system for dietary uses. Freeze-dried meals consist of food that has been quickly frozen and then dried by sucking out the water with a special high-powered vacuum pump. The meals are stored in packets and require no refrigeration. Ochoa notes that dining aboard the shuttle is far different from the liquefied food astronauts ate during earlier times. Whereas astronauts used to squeeze food out of tubes, they now add water to the freeze-dried food and have a more nourishing meal.

One aspect of eating in orbit remains unchanged, however. Food is often tasteless. This is because weightlessness causes a fluid shift in astronauts' heads, making it feel as if they have a head cold, complete with a dulling of the sense of taste. To overcome this, most of the astronauts choose to bring spicy foods into space so that they enjoy at least some flavor when they eat. So desperate are they to experience some taste sensation that a few space travelers even put hot taco sauce on their cereal.

While Ochoa could choose from more than seventy different types of food and twenty different powdered drinks, she could not enjoy cookies or anything else that produced crumbs when handled. In the weightlessness of orbit, loose debris even as tiny as a speck of food can float about the cabin and damage the ultrasensitive equipment aboard the shuttle. As a further safeguard, the astronauts carefully store all trash and bring it back to Earth with them.

# Sleeping

Like all astronauts aboard a shuttle, Ochoa had difficulty sleeping the first few nights in the weightless environment. Sleeping areas are selected by rank, with the shuttle commander having first choice for his or her location, then the next crew member in rank, on down to the lowest rank. The most desirable spots—a corner to squeeze into, a place that has some space, a location where they can feel something against their backs—go fast. The astronaut then secures him- or herself to the area and enjoys some rest. Ochoa compares the sleeping accommodations to squeezing into a coffin or sleeping bag confined to a wall with hooks.

Most astronauts enjoy the sensation that sleeping in a weightless environment produces. Without any pressure against their bodies, they feel as if they are drifting about the sky.

When they have the time to rest and escape from the intense duties that fill their time, the astronauts enjoy gazing at Earth. Ochoa was stunned the first time she looked at her home planet, which emitted a splendid array of startling colors, terrain detail, and brightness beyond description. The planet seemed to glow as if it contained a giant lightbulb inside. "The opportunity to view the Earth from space is just spectacular," Ochoa explained in a magazine article. "It's the one thing we all miss when we return to Earth. Even though we can bring back wonderful pictures and movies it is never quite like being up there personally."[44]

Ochoa recalls how on one of her missions, the crew halted their chores to look at the Aurora Australis, or the Southern Lights, which is an unusual illumination caused by solar wind passing through the upper atmosphere. The spectacle stretched for 1,000 miles (1,609km) from the tip of South America to Antarctica, reminding some of a long, shimmering green snake. Ochoa was as impressed as anyone aboard. She explained the scene to the *Science Teacher* magazine:

> The limb of Earth was behind the Station, and as we
> neared the most southern part of our orbit, we wit-

# Love of Flying

In a NASA interview, astronaut Steven Smith, a member of the STS-110 crew with Ellen Ochoa, talked about how he wound up in the nation's space program. Like many young boys in the 1960s, he immediately fell in love watching the Apollo program.

I was one of those children that, growing up, loved airplanes, and would watch the airplanes take off and land from San Jose International Airport with my mom and dad, who would take us out there to watch the airplanes take off and land. But, about in the mid-'60s, of course, the Apollo program was starting to get into full swing, and that would be broadcast on TV and that really captured my attention, just watching those spacewalks and space flights on the television. I liked it so much, in fact, that when my dad would bring home a Polaroid camera from work, I would sit in front of the TV and take pictures of the TV of the spacewalkers on the moon, not knowing that NASA sold those pictures, also, but I had my own source of them and I still have those pictures, as a matter of fact.

Quoted in NASA, "Preflight Interview with Steven Smith," STS-110. http://spaceflight.nasa.gov/shuttle/archives/sts-110/crew/intsmith.html.

nessed the Southern lights. Ghostly green filaments stretched tens if not hundreds of kilometers into space in ever-changing patterns, with some red bursts of color at the tips. This beautiful, eerie sight mesmerized the crew. Suddenly it was sunrise, and the whole station turned a brilliant white and gold as if a cloaking device had just been removed. It was an incredible moment, not just because of what we saw but whom we saw it with. Working so closely with a team to accomplish a challenging, meaningful task is the greatest reward of being an astronaut.[45]

Another astronaut gazed out the window toward Earth when he saw a meteorite race below him to Earth. "This is too much,"[46] Steve Nagel recalled thinking upon witnessing the incident.

*Ochoa poses with her son Wilson Miles-Ochoa. Being separated from family is one of the challenges of an astronaut's career.*

# Family

While space travel offers the astronauts much, such as the spectacular views, it also contains hardships that Ochoa and her colleagues must deal with. The largest one concerns family, from which she is often separated for long periods of time. Her husband and their two sons watch from a distance as Ochoa participates in exciting missions that thrill the nation. Ochoa misses her husband and children, but she takes comfort in knowing that many other mothers have careers requiring time away from loved ones.

Despite the separations, Ochoa does not want anyone to feel sorry for her, knowing as she does that she is living out a dream by being part of the NASA program. In an interview in 2004 she said:

> I guess I don't see that I sacrificed anything because I've done what I wanted to do. You know, any woman who has a career, when you get married, somehow the two people have to work out when different career opportunities come up for one or the other. And when you have children you have to figure out how you do day care and how you take care of your kids. It's really something that any woman in any career faces.[47]

Ochoa developed activities that helped her sons feel her presence, even as she was being whisked through the skies at top speed. Knowing that young children have little concept of time beyond a day, she decided not to tell them that she would be gone a week or two. Instead she made a paper chain with a link for each day of her mission. By removing one link from the chain every twenty-four hours, her sons could keep track of when their mother would return.

On an earlier mission Ochoa made a tape for the boys to watch. She included the children playing with her, and each night their father played the tape for them. Besides those techniques, when in space Ochoa maintained correspondence with her sons and husband by emailing and, if the mission lasted longer than ten days, through a private video conference set up by NASA.

# Reentry

As the missions near their end, Ochoa and her fellow crew members prepare for reentry and landing. During the final orbit around Earth, they secure all the equipment, put on their launch and reentry suits, and strap themselves to their seats.

The three-stage return takes one hour. In the first phase, the commander executes an upside-down, backward-facing engine burn to slow the shuttle and drop it out of orbit. The onboard computer takes over in the second stage, in which the shuttle descends through the thin upper atmosphere in slow S turns, similar to a skier moving down a slope. An immense flame, caused by friction, engulfs the shuttle during this period and produces charged air particles, called plasma, that create a pink glow. For those on board, the sight is both spectacular and scary. As the loss of the shuttle *Columbia* demonstrated years later, a break in the orbiter's heat-resistant tiles can result in a fire that will consume the shuttle and everyone aboard.

The pilot takes over the controls for the final stage—the actual landing. He bears total responsibility for maneuvering the craft, which is now like a huge glider descending to Earth. Ochoa and the rest of the crew can do nothing but sit and watch. When the shuttle touches down, a 40-foot-diameter drag parachute (12m) opens and helps bring the shuttle to a halt.

Once on Earth, Ochoa and the other astronauts have to deal with the opposite of weightlessness—the pull of Earth's gravity. They feel heavier than normal and sometimes have difficulty with their balance. This dissipates quickly, however, and they are soon able to return to their routines.

As is evident, space travel had much to offer Ochoa. She considered herself fortunate to have flown in space—not once, but twice. In 1999 she again headed toward the stars in her third mission.

# Chapter 5

# "A Field of Opportunities"

In the years that followed her first two space flights, Ochoa would perform other important duties for NASA. She always had training and studying to do in preparation for her next mission, but as the launch might not occur for months or years, she had time for additional duties. She filled that time by assisting fellow astronauts as they prepared for their missions and by speaking to various civic groups about the benefits to society of space exploration.

## Encouragement for Hispanic Americans

Based at the Johnson Space Center in Houston, Texas, Ochoa continued to work as a spacecraft communicator in Mission Control, a job that consisted of relaying instructions to astronauts in orbit; as a software inspector; and as a crew representative in the robotics department. She also labored for two years as an assistant to the chief of the astronaut office, where she utilized her experience and know-how to help other astronauts involved in docking with the International Space Station (ISS).

In many ways the other tasks she carries out are as important as her duties as a NASA employee, for they help assure that young people will consider training for careers with NASA. She is most particularly interested in spreading the word to Hispanic women.

"There's a field of opportunities for Hispanic women in space," said Ochoa, the only female Hispanic astronaut in NASA, to *Hispanic* magazine in 2003. "The key is learning more about what jobs are available out there, what kinds of things you do when you are on the job, and what kind of education you need to get in order to get those jobs. When I started college I didn't select physics right away, partly because I had no idea what a physicist would do."[48]

Ochoa talks to audiences filled with young Hispanic Americans and explains that NASA has more than two thousand Hispanic employees, many of them in electronic, aeronautical, and space

*Astronauts Ellen Ochoa, Joan Higgenbotham, Yvonne Cagle, and Sally Ride (left to right) speak at a symposium at Kennedy Space Center.*

engineering. She adds that 8 out of the 109 NASA astronauts are of Hispanic descent. She mentions the Hispanic inventors, test pilots, mathematicians, and engineers employed by NASA and points to them as an example for the nation's largest minority group. Ochoa notes with sadness that, while Hispanic Americans are increasing in numbers, as a group they have the lowest rate among minorities of earning college degrees in space sciences.

"Obviously, Latinos, and specially women, haven't entered science and technology fields to the degree that other groups have," she explained in 2004, "so I think it's even more important for me to do that, just to get the word out that there are lots of interesting and challenging careers out there when you study math and science. It just opens up a complete world of opportunity when you study those fields."[49]

# The Importance of Reading

In an interview with NASA, astronaut Rex Walheim, who flew with Ellen Ochoa on the STS-110 mission, explained the factors that motivated him to seek a career in space travel:

I started thinking about flying in space when I was a little kid. I used to read fiction books about kids who built their own spacecraft and went to this planet, and so I enjoyed reading about it from a very young age. And that's kind of what got the bug for me. But it was also tied closely to the flying, because I wanted to fly, and I used to go to air shows with my father and my family, and used to love watching the airplanes fly over my house in San Carlos, California. And so that's kind of built upon that, and that's where I started taking the interest in the technical background—the science and the math—and following that through high school, and then getting into engineering school because I thought that was a good background to have in the aviation field.

Quoted in NASA, "Preflight Interview with Rex Walheim," STS-110. http://spaceflight.nasa.gov/shuttle/archives/sts-110/crew/intwalheim.html.

When people ask what route a Hispanic American should take if he or she hopes to join NASA, Ochoa points to the value of a good education. "First of all, I think the key to me getting the job was my education, so studying math and science, going on to college, majoring in some sort of technical career, some field of science, engineering or medicine. Those are sort of the basic requisites that astronauts have."[50]

## A Remarkable Woman

[Ellen Ochoa is] a remarkable woman whose achievements are truly the stuff of legends, but who still thinks of herself as a woman just doing her job. Ellen Ochoa is the epitome of what Latino women can achieve with discipline and determination.

Wendy Pedrero, "Leaders in Space: Conquering the Final Frontier," *Latino Leaders*, October 1, 2004. www.latinoleaders.com/articulos.php?id_sec=1&id_art=89&num_page=273.

Ochoa emphasizes that other skills are also vital, such as understanding how to work as part of a team and understanding one's own strengths and weaknesses as well as other people's strengths and weaknesses. She asserts that a good astronaut knows how to best utilize those qualities in solving problems that may arise in space.

Although she values the benefits offered by the space program, Ochoa notes that other fulfilling careers await bright, determined individuals. She emphasizes the need for teachers in particular. "A hallmark of the Latino community is to help one another," she mentioned in an interview in 2002. "If students are interested in a way to give back and help their communities, becoming a teacher is probably one of the very best ways of doing that."[51]

## Another Launch

As valuable as she considered her work as an advocate for NASA to be, especially when talking with Hispanic Americans, Ochoa most wanted to fly in space. It was, after all, why she joined NASA. She had to wait five long years before she enjoyed another opportunity since the 1994 STS-66 mission. At times she wondered if she would ever again enjoy the excitement of a space shuttle flight,

*The crew of the 1999 STS-96 mission, including Ochoa (center), waves to onlookers before departing.*

but her doubts dissipated when she was assigned to the STS-96 mission set from May 27 to June 6, 1999.

The ten-day mission aboard *Discovery* carried seven crew members, including an astronaut from the Canadian Space Agency and another from the Russian Space Agency. Ochoa participated as a mission specialist and flight engineer. The primary missions for the crew were to implement the first docking with the ISS and to transfer supplies from the shuttle to the station. In addition, the astronauts were to conduct an experiment called STARSHINE, which would involve a multinational group of students tracking from their schools the path of a satellite.

Ochoa looked forward to the mission, which incorporated some of the most intricate assignments ever asked of an astronaut. As she explained in a NASA media release, she looked forward to the challenges for a number of reasons:

> One of them is that each flight will involve space walks and moving the robotic arm around and often with very little out-the-window view to be able to see what you're doing. And so that makes it very challenging for the astronauts. Secondly, there's no way to do end-to-end tests of the equipment on the ground because you're launching it in stages. So everyone, the astronauts onboard and the people on the ground, [has] to be prepared for surprises along the way.[52]

*Discovery* rose from its Florida launch pad early in the morning on May 27, 1999. Once in orbit, the astronauts immediately prepared for the first of their complex assignments—the initial docking with the ISS, a joint venture involving nations from Europe, Asia, and North America, so they could transfer badly needed supplies and building materials.

Two days after launch, the crew maneuvered *Discovery* close to the station, with Ochoa keeping track of the shuttle's trajectory as it neared the ISS. While Ochoa observed the distance between the shuttle and the station, astronaut Tammy Jernigan used a laser to help align the shuttle. This laser-guided system also would alert the crew if the shuttle approached on the wrong trajectory. As this was the first time that the shuttle had ever docked with the ISS, everyone was on the alert. The tension among *Discovery*'s crew was higher than normal as the orbiter neared its objective.

Pilot Rick Husband explained details of the mission in a NASA press release shortly before the launch:

> Ellen will be working with a tool that we use for rendezvous and docking called Rendezvous and Proximity Operations Program. And what this thing does is it can show you your trajectory with respect to the station and how you're doing with your burns, your corrections,

and everything. And so it's a tremendous aid and gives us a lot more situational awareness to visualize where we are with respect to the station and how our different burns are doing. Also, Tammy will be working with a hand-held laser and she'll be able to get range and range rate and how fast we're closing with the station from that information. And all those things are incorporated into this program that Ellen is using.[53]

Commander Kent Rominger and Husband kept watch over the shuttle controls while Ochoa and Jernigan relayed information yielded by the laptop computer and laser. As *Discovery* neared the ISS from below, Rominger executed a fly around to position the shuttle above the station. In the final approach, Rominger dropped the shuttle's speed so that it moved only .03 foot per second (.009 meter per second) to successfully complete the docking.

## The Spacewalk

The challenging tasks hardly ended with the intricate docking maneuvers, for the next day the crew had to execute a spacewalk and begin shifting 2 tons (1.8 metric tons) of supplies from the shuttle into the ISS. On May 30, mission specialists Tammy Jernigan and Daniel Barry donned space suits, left the shuttle, and while Ochoa operated the robotic arm from inside *Discovery*, transferred two cranes from the shuttle's payload bay and installed them on the outside of the ISS. These cranes would be used in subsequent missions to help astronauts enlarge or make necessary repairs to the ISS. Jernigan and Barry also installed two portable foot restraints to the outside and attached three bags of tools and handrails for use by future crews.

Ochoa once again performed a task that was critical to the success of this spacewalk. Since the cranes were so large, Jernigan and Barry could not simply maneuver them into place. They needed the robotic arm to do that for them. The pair moved to the end of the arm operated by Ochoa and held onto the cranes, then let Ochoa slowly move them into the proper location. Ochoa had to possess a deft touch in this task, for any false move or error could endanger the astronauts. Once in place, the two astronauts attached the cranes to the station.

The next day the crew began transferring 2 tons (1.8 metric tons) of equipment to the ISS, a process that took several days to complete. These supplies—clothing, computers, medical equipment, water, sleeping bags, spare parts, and so on—would be used by the first crews to actually live for long periods of time in the ISS.

## Beyond Boundaries

As a mission specialist who has traveled to space four times, Ellen has been able to experience the thrill and trepidation of having gone to a place where few men and even fewer women have ever gone before.

Wendy Pedrero, "Leaders in Space: Conquering the Final Frontier," *Latino Leaders*, October 1, 2004. www.latinoleaders.com/articulos.php?id_sec=1&id_art=89&num_page=273.

Ochoa and the other crew members were excited about docking with the ISS, as they knew their work would help maintain the momentum that was building for missions involving travel deeper into space. Their work would create a home for future astronauts, one with food, water, air, and everything else a human being needs to survive. "But this is almost the last step in a very long process of developing a piece of hardware that is incredible in its performance," said Barry before the mission. "Think about what we're planning to do with the station: it's really our stepping stone to Mars. We're going to learn how to live and work long-term in space. We're going to learn how to keep people healthy up there for long periods of time."[54]

Using the robotic arm to transfer the supplies was more difficult for Ochoa than her previous uses of the equipment had been. In the other missions, in which she deployed and retrieved satellites, she had only had to perform brief moves and then only once or twice. But to transfer supplies from the payload bay to the ISS, she had to perform precise operations many times over several days. Making her task more demanding was that she had no clear view of the robotic arm or the astronaut working at the end of the arm. Since they were docked to the ISS, Ochoa's views outside her window were blocked by the station itself. This forced

# The International Space Station

Like Ellen Ochoa, Daniel Barry participated in shuttle missions that brought supplies to the International Space Station. In an interview with NASA, Barry explained the important role the space station will play:

> I don't think we're going to go to Mars as the United States. I think we're going to go to Mars as people from Earth. So that, to me, is a significant goal of the station, learning how to work as a crew from Earth, not a crew from the United States. We have different languages on Earth; we have different cultures on Earth; that's going to need to become unified in space. There are other applications, probably too many to list: looking at pharmaceuticals, looking at material properties, learning about thermodynamic parts of materials, we have just all kinds of what I would call smaller specific applications of this unique environment. You have a chance to be in free fall, to not have gravity pulling you down. You can see lots of effects that you can't see in an Earth environment. But I think we're doing those, sort of at the same time as we're doing, to me, the bigger issue, which is preparing to go to Mars.

Quoted in NASA, "Preflight Interview with Daniel Barry," STS-96. http://spaceflight.nasa.gov/shuttle/archives/sts-96/crew/intbarry.html.

*Astronaut Tammy Jernigan performs a space walk as part of the STS-96 mission, which carried supplies to the International Space Station.*

her to rely on a video monitor and information provided by the astronauts outside. Ochoa could not afford to bump the arm against any solid object, which might have damaged the arm or endangered the astronauts, or stretch the arm so far that the joints could no longer move properly.

"As a matter of fact," Rominger said in an interview with NASA, "early in the mission this was something I underestimated the complexity of. Her [Ochoa's] task is made much more difficult because you can't see much."[55]

Over the next four days Ochoa methodically followed an extensive checklist to ensure she transferred the materials to the ISS in the proper order. Using the robotic arm, she unbuckled each piece of equipment, removed it from its storage rack, then shifted it over to the space station. As Ochoa performed her duties, other astronauts stowed the material in the proper location in the ISS. At the end of each day, Ochoa compared her checklist with the one maintained by the astronauts stowing the materials, then informed ground control in Houston what had been transferred.

## STARSHINE Project

As she had done during her other shuttle missions, Ochoa found time to communicate with the press and to work with students on Earth. On June 1, Ochoa, Rominger, and Husband were interviewed by *Good Morning America* and by television reporters from stations in Texas and Colorado. The object of these interviews was to garner favorable publicity for NASA and to promote the idea of future space exploration.

Even more important for Ochoa was having another opportunity to work with high school students from around the world. In a project called STARSHINE, which a professor at the University of Utah designed, Ochoa placed in orbit a basketball-size satellite bearing nine hundred aluminum mirrors. Each mirror was polished and prepared by the students at a different school, then sent to NASA's laboratories in Houston to be mounted on the satellite. More than twenty-five thousand students from eighteen nations, using orbital mechanics, then tracked the satellite as it moved through the heavens. Students were able to see the satellite during sunrise and sunset, depending upon the time and the particular orbit.

NASA set up the program so that by way of a Web site the students could share their information with other students around the world. By observing the changes in the satellite's orbit over a six-month period as it slowed and dropped lower to Earth's atmosphere, they were able to determine the atmospheric drag effects on the orb. The immense project asked students to utilize mathematical knowledge, make careful observations, and communicate with other students around the globe.

"It's a collaborative international project that will bring students together where they've managed to touch the hardware and then will see it go by in the sky until it reenters the atmosphere," mission specialist Julie Payette said before the mission. "I think it's extraordinary. We'll make new astronauts and rocket scientists out of those bunches for sure."[56]

*Ochoa works with Valery Tokarev, a Russian cosmonaut who participated in the STS-96 mission.*

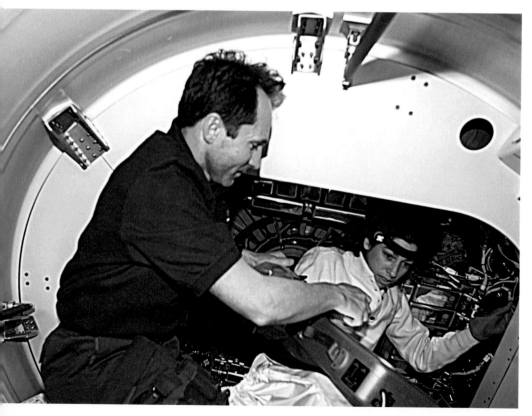

# Cola Wars in Space

The cola war pitting Coca-Cola versus Pepsi-Cola exists even in space. Coca-Cola received permission from NASA to conduct an experiment in space to see if it could properly dispense carbonated beverages, which produce bubbles, in zero gravity. Coca-Cola built a special can for the experiment.

Before the company had a chance to send the can into orbit during a shuttle mission, Pepsi-Cola learned of the experiment and demanded that it be able to send its own version of a space can on the same mission. NASA agreed and gave time for Pepsi-Cola to develop its own can.

Pepsi-Cola's insistence on being given an opportunity did not help. Astronauts found that Coca-Cola's can produced fewer bubbles.

## Back to Earth

Deploying the satellite for the STARSHINE Project fulfilled one of the main objectives of STS-96. On June 3, Husband undocked *Discovery* from the ISS, circled the station twice, then fired the jets to move *Discovery* away from the station. As Husband steered the shuttle, Ochoa monitored a computer monitor that kept track of the undocking process, then used a program on her laptop computer to plot the shuttle's trajectory.

On June 5 *Discovery's* cargo bay doors swung shut. Once that was completed, Ochoa and the others donned their launch and reentry suits, strapped themselves into their seats, and prepared for the return home.

*Discovery* successfully landed at Kennedy Space Center in Florida on June 6, after completing a journey of 4 million miles (6.4 million km). Physicians put Ochoa and the other crew members through routine medical examinations, then released the weary astronauts so they could be reunited with their families.

Despite the triumphs of STS-96, and despite the fact that she had flown on three missions, Ochoa's experiences in space were not at an end. She had one more trip to make. After that, a bright future with NASA loomed, one that she hoped would include still more trips into the startling realm of space.

## Chapter 6

# "Mommy, Can Boys Be Astronauts, Too?"

For Ochoa, each time she soared toward the heavens it seemed that she faced more demanding tasks. On her fourth flight into space, she again directed the robotic arm, but this time she used it to move giant construction materials from the shuttle to the ISS and to move astronauts through space. The complexities of these operations made the earlier deployment of satellites seem tame, but Ochoa handled the work with efficiency.

## STS-110

Ochoa encountered another delay when the scheduled launch date of April 4, 2002, for STS-110 had to be changed. A hydrogen leak caused Mission Control to halt the countdown and set a new target of April 8. Operations unfolded smoothly on that day, and the shuttle *Atlantis* carried Ochoa and six other astronauts, including three shuttle rookies, into orbit.

The main task for STS-110 was to deliver and attach to the ISS a huge array of solar panels that would add more power to the station so that it could expand its laboratory space. Operating the robotic arm, Ochoa moved the 43-foot-long, 27,000-pound structure (13m, 12,247kg) into place, where its solar panels began providing additional power.

The solar equipment contained numerous features. "It's hexagonal in cross section," Ochoa explained in a NASA interview, "and the width and the height are about fourteen feet each. If you get close to SO [the designation for the structure] you realize that it's covered with equipment. It has computers, it has fluid lines, miles of cable, almost a thousand electrical connections."[57]

In two spacewalks, Ochoa and her fellow astronauts attached the unit to the ISS. Ochoa moved the astronauts, anchored to the robotic arm, through space as they bolted the structure to the space station.

*Ochoa, far right, joins other members of the crew of the STS-110 mission for a photograph at NASA.*

*This 1976 photo, taken by the* Viking I *spacecraft, shows the surface of Mars. Future space missions will likely focus on the exploration of this planet.*

Besides attaching the power structure, Ochoa again supervised the transfer of supplies to the ISS. She sent over equipment for new science experiments and brought back equipment from other experiments that had been concluded. She then transferred laptop computers, water, and other necessary materials.

The astronauts had time for a bit of fun during this eleven-day mission. Between the two spacewalks that were required for attaching the solar panels, Mission Control in Houston gave the crew an afternoon off. As it was rodeo season back in Texas, the crew planned an elaborate barbecue with the occupants of the ISS, astronauts from Russia and Japan. With country music playing in the background, the two crews shared a memorable meal.

"One of the fun things we did on my last flight," Ochoa said later, "was host a space food meal on our shuttle for another station crew that was up there at the time. We brought a Texas meal with barbecue beef, mashed potatoes and corn, and the station crew shared a buffet of Russian and Japanese food. That was one of the social highlights of the mission."[58]

*Atlantis* returned to Kennedy Space Center on April 19, after completing 171 orbits of Earth, the equivalent of traveling a distance of 4.5 million miles (7.3 million km). Ochoa, now one of the most experienced astronauts in the crew, had flown nearly one thousand hours in space in her four missions.

Ochoa hoped to add to that total, but at this point disaster caused a long delay in the shuttle program. The shuttle *Columbia* disintegrated upon reentry from its flight on February 1, 2003, killing the seven astronauts aboard. Following the accident, NASA grounded the entire shuttle fleet for a three-year period while it looked for the cause of the crash. By the time NASA resumed shuttle flights with the June 2006 launch of *Discovery*, Ochoa's hopes for future flights dimmed. No one could tell how many, if any, future shuttle missions would be conducted.

# The Future

While waiting for assignment to another mission, Ochoa performs other duties for NASA. She is currently the deputy director of Flight Crew Operations, the unit that manages and directs the Astronaut Office and the Aircraft Operations Division at Johnson Space Center in Houston. In this job, she and the director are responsible for training crew members for space flights and for bringing crew-member experience and knowledge to bear in order to solve problems that arise in the space program. Ochoa's specific job is to supervise flight simulation and training programs and to record the progress of astronauts involved in those activities.

Ochoa hopes to fly on more missions before retiring to do something calmer. "Maybe at some point I will try something new," she said in 2003, "but I am enjoying it and I hope to fly more in the future."[59]

She realizes, however, that her chances are slimmer now than they were earlier. The shuttle program is due to be retired in 2010, as the focus of space exploration returns to lunar landings and voyages to Mars. NASA is concentrating on training the astronauts who will be responsible for this next phase of space exploration.

"If these are really the exploration astronauts," said Rominger in 2006, who now makes flight assignments, "I need to get them on another space vehicle first."[60] Since half of the one hundred members of the astronaut corps have yet to experience space flight, and with a maximum of only seventeen shuttle flights remaining, Rominger has made some tough calls. To give training to those who need it most, Rominger has grounded veterans with four or more space flights, a group that includes Ochoa.

## "It's a Spirit of Adventure"

Even if she never again enjoys the thrill of rocketing into outer space, Ochoa feels fortunate to have been a part of what she considers a significant endeavor. She believes, as do her fellow astronauts, that she has contributed to an amazing saga. One of Ochoa's colleagues says they are driven by the same impulse that prodded others to explore the New World in previous centuries.

"I think it's the same thing that drove people across this continent when they first came here, from east to west," claimed Jerry Ross, who flew with Ochoa in STS-110. "It's a spirit of adventure. It's a—what's over the next hill, what's beyond that next planet—the same type of thing."[61]

Ochoa is an enthusiastic proponent of the International Space Station. When people question how the shuttle program or the ISS helps the nation, or they criticize NASA for a lack of vision, she is ready with counterarguments:

> I see really three main roles that the International Space Station plays in future exploration. One of these is that much of the research is directed at Earth. We'll be looking at medical advances, at new materials research, at environmental sensing. So we're going to be learning about a lot of new technologies in that sense and they should benefit people here on Earth.
>
> Secondly, we're using it to test technologies that can be used when we advance human space exploration, including possible trips to the moon or Mars.

# Many Awards

Ellen Ochoa has received many awards for the work she has done in promoting the space program and in providing a positive role model for the nation's youth. In 1995 NASA gave her the Outstanding Leadership Medal, followed by the Exceptional Service Medal two years later. She received Space Flight Medals in 1999 and 2002, and her alma mater, San Diego State University, honored her with the Alumna of the Year Award. In March 2003 Ochoa became the first honoree for the 2003 Women's History Month, a time designated to recognize the contributions to society made by females.

Reflective of her pride in her Hispanic background, Ochoa has received the Albert Baez Award for Outstanding Contribution to Humanity and the Hispanic Heritage Leadership Award. One significant honor was being selected in 1999 by President Bill Clinton to serve on the Presidential Commission on the Celebration of Women in American History.

*Ochoa, shown here with some of her crewmates on the STS-66 mission, has won many prestigious awards.*

*Scientists hope that research performed on board the International Space Station will lead to advances both in space travel and in new technologies on Earth.*

And third, it's really leading the way in terms of international cooperation where countries are all working together focused on a common goal that benefits people around the world. And I'm sure that will be a hallmark of all future exploration activities as well.[62]

## "Reach for the Stars"

While Ochoa waits for the chance, however slim, to fly again, she continues her work for NASA, both at Houston and around the country. She gains the greatest satisfaction from visiting schools and speaking to students about their futures and what it takes to make it in society.

"I've probably given 150 talks over the past few years," said Ochoa recently. "I never thought about this aspect of the job when I was applying [to become an astronaut], but it's extremely rewarding. I'm not trying to make every kid an astronaut, but I want kids to think about a career and the preparation they'll need."[63]

Ochoa leaves Johnson Space Center at least once a month to meet with students and spread her message. NASA has made a serious commitment to informing young people about the space program and to present its personnel as positive role models for the nation's youth. Ochoa tells them to set goals and then work hard to attain those goals. She explains that the success she has enjoyed began with a solid education, and she urges them to start figuring out what they want to do in the future. Above all, she encourages them to aim for lofty goals.

# Motivation Is Important

Mike Bloomfield, an astronaut who flew with Ellen Ochoa in the STS-110 flight in 2002, explained in a NASA interview what attracted him to the agency:

> Well, I'm very fortunate to be wrapped up in this. I remember when I first came to NASA for an interview on whether or not I wanted to be an astronaut, and I wasn't convinced that's what I wanted to do. And I came down here for the interview process, kind of checking NASA out as well, is this someplace I really want to go; and the thing that struck me when I came down here was how dedicated the people were to their job, how motivated they were, and how excited they were about space travel. And, I go, I want to go there because here's a lot of people that enjoy learning new things, they enjoy doing new things. When we go do this mission we, there's just a group of seven of us and three on the station so there's ten of us up there, but there are literally thousands of people down here on Earth that are supporting us. And they have supported us since we started training; in many cases they were working on this mission for four or five years before we even [showed] up. So we're a very small part of this whole thing. What we're doing is a result of the incredible teamwork that takes place here at NASA. And so I feel very fortunate to be just a small part of that tremendous team.

Quoted in NASA, "Preflight Interview with Michael Bloomfield," STS-110. http://spaceflight.nasa.gov/shuttle/archives/sts-110/crew/intbloomfield.html.

Ochoa finds that depending on her audience, which may consist of middle school students or college seniors, the questions she is asked vary. Younger students generally want to know how astronauts eat, sleep, work, and go to the bathroom in space, whereas the high school and college students ask questions that go beyond that. They usually inquire about Ochoa's reasons for joining NASA, what her specific roles are with the agency, what she plans to do in the future, and what NASA's plans are for future space exploration.

When a student specifically inquires about what he or she can do to become an astronaut, Ochoa has a ready answer: "Astronauts must have a college degree in a technical field—some area of science, engineering, math, or medicine. Most astronauts have at least a master's degree, and many mission specialists, like me, have either a doctorate or medical degree."[64]

She tells students that achieving high marks in the classroom is not enough by itself. Maturity is highly valued. "Other skills are important too: understanding how to work as part of a team, understanding your own strengths and weaknesses, being able to understand other people's strengths and weaknesses, making the most of your strengths and minimizing your weaknesses. Those are really important to becoming a good astronaut."[65]

Ochoa goes on to explain that NASA seeks people who possess multiple skills and interests and candidates who grasp concepts quickly. NASA also wants astronauts who have an interest in a wide variety of areas and who took part in many extracurricular activities in school.

She often ends with a simple reminder of what she has tried to convey. As she mentioned in an interview in 2006:

> When a student asks me what he or she can do to succeed in life, not only as an astronaut, but in any field, I tell them, "Study hard and stay in school, do your best at whatever you do, set high goals for yourself." Many teamwork and interpersonal skills can be gained as you participate in sports, music, and other activities.[66]

# Hispanic American Women

Because of her ethnicity, Ochoa is sensitive to the needs and hopes of Hispanic American students, especially women. She understands that many Hispanic women look to people like herself, women who have succeeded, as their role models. Ochoa takes that responsibility seriously.

In 2003 the University of Texas–Pan American in Edinburg, Texas, held a weeklong conference that brought prominent Hispanic Americans to the school to inspire South Texas children to enter the fields of mathematics, science, and technology. The students listened to motivational stories from Hispanic women, such as Ochoa and *Latina* magazine publisher Christy Haubegger, who smashed barriers to their success in fields once dominated by men. Ochoa and Haubegger wanted to be for these students what they rarely had when they grow up—a positive role model for Hispanic American females.

## A Role Model

We have a lot of students at the college who are first-generation college students from moderate- to low-income backgrounds who have not had the chance to meet many role models, somebody they can emulate. Ellen Ochoa is someone who has accomplished a lot.

Quoted in Lydia Martin, "Astronaut Is Thrilled by Beauty of Universe," Knight-Ridder/Tribune News Service, December 1, 1993. www.lasmujeres.com/ellenochoa/biography.shtml.

Ochoa urged the females in her audience to challenge themselves and stay in school:

> As you can see space exploration is not a field for ordinary people working ordinary jobs. The development and operation of the space shuttle and space station require a tremendous amount of expertise and dedication from all the people who work on it. An education is what provides these people with the knowledge and tools to do their jobs. These students here can be the ones that develop future space station experiments or

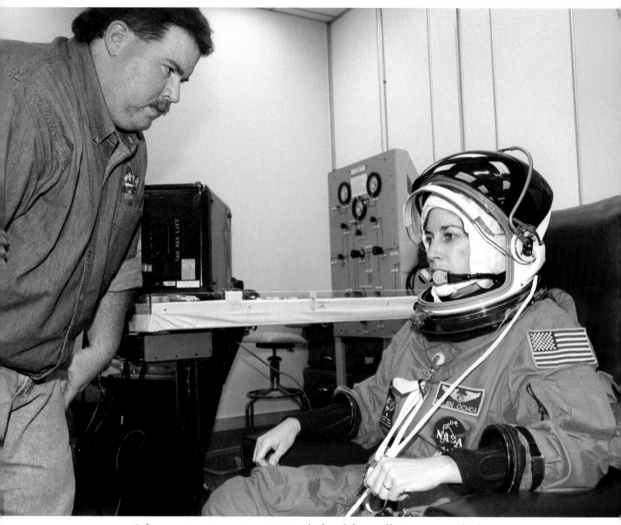

*Ochoa receives intensive training before lifting off into space. She hopes to have another opportunity to travel into space.*

design spacecrafts for Mars. All you have to do is continue your education and choose to succeed.[67]

Ochoa added another important ingredient—the value of family in a person's life. "I think it is important to get the whole family involved. My family, especially my mother, was real important to me early on in stressing the importance of education," Ochoa said. "I hope people can understand how it can lead to real exciting and rewarding careers."[68]

Ochoa's words had an impact on people in the audience, not just younger listeners but their parents as well. Nelinda Villarreal attended the conference with her daughter, Samantha, and said they were moved by the astronaut's words. Nelinda explained that she realized how she as a parent can affect her daughter's life:

> Today I learned how important it is to be a role model for our children and the need to really let them expand their horizons and not hold them back. We as parents a lot of times want to keep our kids close to us, but that can be more of a hindrance than an advantage and so we as parents need to support our children in all aspects and every decision that they make.[69]

At the same time, Samantha walked away with her own lesson. The high school student loved listening to successful Hispanic women relate the stories of their careers and how they faced the obstacles that stood in their way. Samantha added that the speakers motivated her to pursue her goal of becoming a chemical engineer or a doctor. "I learned that education is really important and Hispanics can do anything they want to do,"[70] stated the student.

Those words from Nelinda and Samantha make Ochoa smile. She looks to space when she thinks of her own career, but when she examines the impact of what she does, especially on the nation's young women, her gaze returns to Earth.

Her older son, Wilson, gave her a clear example that the role of women in science is changing from one of almost total exclusion to one of inclusion. "My [preschool] son looked at me one Saturday when we were driving by the Johnson Space Center and asked, 'Mommy, can boys be astronauts, too?' I'm happy to see my boys grow up not having some of the preconceived gender boundaries that a lot of women my age grew up with."[71]

Ochoa intends to continue that work, hopefully in space, but certainly in the classrooms throughout the country.

# Important Dates

**1958**
Born in Los Angeles, California, on May 10.

**1975**
Graduates as class valedictorian from Grossmont High School in La Mesa, California; attends San Diego State University.

**1980**
Graduates as class valedictorian from San Diego State University.

**1981**
Earns a master's degree in science from Stanford University.

**1983**
Sally Ride becomes the first female astronaut to travel in space on June 18.

**1985**
Receives her doctorate in electrical engineering from Stanford University; takes a job as researcher at Sandia National Laboratories.

**1987**
Selected as one of the top one hundred finalists for a position as astronaut.

**1988**
Begins work at NASA's Ames Research Center.

**1990**
In January, is selected to be an astronaut by NASA; marries Coe Fulmer Miles.

**1993**
Participates in her first mission into space, STS-56, which launches on April 8; she and the crew return to Earth on April 17.

**1994**
Participates in her second mission into space, STS-66, which launches on November 3; she and the crew return to Earth on November 14.

**1999**
Participates in her third mission into space, STS-96, which launches on May 27; she and the crew successfully complete the first docking of the shuttle with the International Space Station; she and the crew return to Earth on June 6.

**2002**
Participates in her fourth mission into space, STS-110, which launches on April 8; she and the crew return to Earth on April 19.

# Notes

## Introduction: "There Were No Female Astronauts"

1. Quoted in Megan Sullivan, "An Interview with NASA Astronaut Ellen Ochoa," *Science Teacher*, February 2005. www.nsta.org/main/news/stories/science_teacher.php?news_story_ID=50189.
2. In Anne Hart, "Without Limits," www.graduatingengineer.com/articles/minority/11-12-99.html.

## Chapter 1: "Education Can Open Doors"

3. Quoted in "Meet Famous Latinos—Ellen Ochoa," 1999. www.teacher.scholastic.com/activities/hispanic/ochoatscript.htm.
4. Quoted in Hart, "Without Limits."
5. Quoted in Stanford University School of Engineering, "Ellen Ochoa: A Higher Education." http://soe.stanford.edu/AR97-98/ochoa.html.
6. Quoted in NASA, "Preflight Interview with Ellen Ochoa," STS-110. http://spaceflight.nasa.gov/shuttle/archives/sts-110/crew/intochoa.html.
7. Quoted in NASA, "Preflight Interview with Ellen Ochoa," STS-96. http://spaceflight.nasa.gov/shuttle/archives/sts-96/crew/intochoa.html.
8. Written response to author's query, May 26, 2006.
9. Quoted in "Dr. Ellen Ochoa: Education—The Stepping Stone to the Stars," *La Prensa San Diego*, December 7, 2001. www.laprensa-sandiego.org/archieve/december07/ochoa.htm.
10. Quoted in Womenworking.com, "Star-Trekking: Ellen Ochoa." www.womenworking2000.com/feature/index.php?id=81.

11. Quoted in NASA, "Preflight Interview with Ellen Ochoa," STS-110.
12. Quoted in NASA, "Preflight Interview with Ellen Ochoa," STS-110.
13. Written response to author's query, May 26, 2006.
14. Quoted in "Meet Dr. Ellen Ochoa: Dr. Ochoa's Biographical Sketch." www.smithsonianeducation.org/scitech/impacto/graphic/ellen/biography.html.

## Chapter 2: "Being Prepared for a Great Adventure"

15. Quoted in NASA, "Preflight Interview with Ellen Ochoa," STS-96.
16. Written response to author's query, May 26, 2006.
17. Quoted in Angela Posada-Swafford, "A Place in the Stars," *Hispanic*, June 2003. www.hispaniconline.com/magazine/2003/june/Features/leading-ellen.html#top.
18. Quoted in "Meet Dr. Ellen Ochoa."
19. Quoted in Lydia Martin, "Astronaut Is Thrilled by Beauty of Universe," Knight-Ridder/Tribune News Service, December 1, 1993. www.lasmujeres.com/ellenochoa/biography.shtml.
20. Written response to author's query, May 26, 2006.
21. Written response to author's query, May 26, 2006.
22. Written response to author's query, May 26, 2006.
23. Written response to author's query, May 26, 2006.

## Chapter 3: "What Engineer Wouldn't Want Those Experiences?"

24. Written response to author's query, May 26, 2006.
25. Written response to author's query, May 26, 2006.
26. Quoted in Hart, "Without Limits."
27. Quoted in Miles O'Brien, "Getting to Know the Crew of STS-96," CNN.com, May 24, 1999. www.cnn.com/TECH/space/9905/24/downlinks/#2.
28. Quoted in O'Brien, "Getting to Know the Crew of STS-96."
29. Quoted in "Atlantis Shuttle Mission, STS-66 Inflight Crew

Portrait." www.smithsonianeducation.org/scitech/ impacto/ Text2/ellen/atlantis_sts66.html.

30. Quoted in NASA, "STS-66." http://science.ksc.nasa.gov/shut tle/missions/sts-66/mission-sts66.html.

31. Quoted in Tony Reichhardt, *Space Shuttle: The First 20 Years.* Washington, DC.: Smithsonian Institution, 2002, p. 81.

32. Quoted in Stanford University School of Engineering, "Ellen Ochoa."

33. Quoted in Hart, "Without Limits."

34. Quoted in Hart, "Without Limits."

35. Quoted in NASA, "STS-66."

36. Quoted in NASA, "STS-66."

## Chapter 4: "Going into Space Is Very Exciting"

37. Quoted in Reichhardt, *Space Shuttle*, p. 61.

38. Quoted in Sullivan, "An Interview with NASA Astronaut Ellen Ochoa."

39. Quoted in Reichhardt, *Space Shuttle*, p. 145.

40. Quoted in Reichhardt, *Space Shuttle*, p. 146.

41. Quoted in Sullivan, "An Interview with NASA Astronaut Ellen Ochoa."

42. Quoted in Reichhardt, *Space Shuttle*, p. 161.

43. Quoted in Reichhardt, *Space Shuttle*, p. 39.

44. Quoted in Wendy Pedrero, "Leaders in Space: Conquering the Final Frontier," *Latino Leaders*, October 1, 2004. www.latino leaders.com/articulos.php?id_sec=1&id_art=89&num_page= 273.

45. Quoted in Sullivan, "An Interview with NASA Astronaut Ellen Ochoa."

46. Quoted in Reichhardt, *Space Shuttle*, p. 179.

47. Quoted in Pedrero, "Leaders in Space."

## Chapter 5: "A Field of Opportunities"

48. Quoted in Posada-Swafford, "A Place in the Stars."

49. Quoted in Pedrero, "Leaders in Space."

50. Quoted in Pedrero, "Leaders in Space."

51. Quoted in "Dr. Ellen Ochoa: Education—The Stepping Stone to the Stars."
52. Quoted in NASA, "Preflight Interview with Ellen Ochoa," STS-96.
53. Quoted in NASA, "Preflight Interview with Rick Husband," STS-96. http://spaceflight.nasa.gov/shuttle/archives/sts-96/crew/inthusband.html.
54. Quoted in NASA, "Preflight Interview with Daniel Barry," STS-96. http://spaceflight.nasa.gov/shuttle/archives/sts-96/crew/intbarry.html.
55. Quoted in NASA, "Preflight Interview with Kent Rominger," STS-96. http://spaceflight.nasa.gov/shuttle/archives/sts-96/crew/introminger.html.
56. Quoted in NASA, "Preflight Interview with Julie Payette," STS-96. http://spaceflight.nasa.gov/shuttle/archives/sts-96/crew/intpayette.html.

## Chapter 6: "Mommy, Can Boys Be Astronauts, Too?"

57. Quoted in NASA, "Preflight Interview with Ellen Ochoa," STS-110.
58. Quoted in Womenworking.com, "Star-Trekking: Ellen Ochoa."
59. Quoted in Posada-Swafford, "A Place in the Stars."
60. Quoted in Chris Kridler, "Astronauts Caught in NASA's Big Transition," *Detroit Free Press*, May 31, 2006, p. 8A.
61. Quoted in NASA, "Preflight Interview with Jerry Ross," STS-110. http://spaceflight.nasa.gov/shuttle/archives/sts-110/crew/intross.html.
62. Quoted in NASA, "Preflight Interview with Ellen Ochoa," STS-96.
63. Quoted in Stanford University School of Engineering, "Ellen Ochoa."
64. Quoted in Sullivan, "An Interview with NASA Astronaut Ellen Ochoa."
65. Quoted in Pedrero, "Leaders in Space."
66. Written response to author's query, May 26, 2006.
67. Quoted in Office of University Relations, University of

Texas–Pan American, "Latina Day During HESTIC Brings Inspiration to Young Women." www.utpa.edu/news/index.cfm?newsid=2586&curtype=release&curbar=news.

68. Quoted in Office of University Relations, University of Texas–Pan American, "Latina Day During HESTIC Brings Inspiration to Young Women."

69. Quoted in Office of University Relations, University of Texas–Pan American, "Latina Day During HESTIC Brings Inspiration to Young Women."

70. Quoted in Office of University Relations, University of Texas–Pan American, "Latina Day During HESTIC Brings Inspiration to Young Women."

71. Quoted in Womenworking.com, "Star-Trekking: Ellen Ochoa."

# For More Information

## Books

Tony Reichhardt, *Space Shuttle: The First 20 Years*. Washington, DC: Smithsonian Institution, 2002. This superb book offers a fascinating glimpse into life aboard a space shuttle, mainly through interviews with many astronauts.

## Magazines and Newspapers

*Hispanic Times Magazine*, "Dr. Ellen Ochoa: Education—The Stepping Stone to the Stars," Spring, 2002, This article focuses on Ochoa's educational and family backgrounds.

Chris Kridler, "Astronauts Caught in NASA's Big Transition," *Detroit Free Press*, May 31, 2006. Kridler's article spells out what the change in space exploration, from shuttle launching to deep space exploration, could mean to Ochoa and other veterans of the shuttle program.

Wendy Pedrero, "The Sky's the Limit," *Latino Leaders*, October-November 2004, Pedrero offers some good material on how Ochoa balances family responsibilities with her space work.

Angela Posada-Swafford, "A Place in the Stars," *Hispanic Magazine*, June 2003. This brief article contains some useful information on Ochoa's family and on the value of her work for Hispanic Americans.

Traci Watson, "NASA's Mission: Keep Vultures from Shuttle Launch Pad," *Detroit Free Press*, June 9, 2006, p. 10A. The article tells about the drastic measures NASA had to adopt to keep vultures and other birds away from the shuttle launch pad.

## Internet Sources

"Atlantis Shuttle Mission, STS-66 Inflight Crew Portrait." www. smithsonianeducation.org/scitech/impacto/Text2/ellen/atlantis_ sts66.html. This material provides background on Ochoa and other astronauts.

"Dr. Ochoa's Biographical Sketch." www.smithsonianedu cation.org/scitech/impacto/graphic/ellen/biography.html. This material provides background on Ochoa and offers sound recordings of brief interviews with her.

"Ellen Ochoa." www.gale.com/free_resources/chh/bio/ochoa_e. htm. This three-page biography provides a succinct summary of the astronaut's life and gives the reader a decent place to start learning about her contributions.

"Ellen Ochoa." www.nwhp.org/tlp/biographies/ochoa/ochoa_ bio.html. The National Women's History Project honored Ochoa for furthering the place of females in society. The organization published this short biography of the astronaut.

"Ellen Ochoa." http://soe.stanford.edu/AR97-98/ochoa.html, Stanford University published this profile of one of its most renowned graduates. It is an excellent brief summary of her life.

Anne Hart, "Without Limits." www.graduatingengineer.com/arti cles/minority/11-12-99.html. Hart assembles a very good portrait of Ellen Ochoa that includes information on her educational background and on her first three missions.

Lydia Martin, "Astronaut Is Thrilled by Beauty of Universe," Knight-Ridder/Tribune News Service, December 1, 1993. www.lasmujeres.com/ellenochoa/biography.shtml. Martin offers comments on the importance of Hispanic American contributions to society.

"Meet Famous Latinos—Ellen Ochoa." www.teacher.scholastic. com/activities/hispanic/ochoascript.htm. In 1999 *Scholastic* magazine conducted this enlightening interview with Ellen Ochoa. She talks about her incentives to be an astronaut and urges students to work hard and have dreams.

Miles O'Brien, "Getting to Know the Crew of STS-96," CNN.com, May 24, 1999. www.cnn.com/TECH/space/9905/24/down links/#2. O'Brien's article provides brief introductions to the crew members of STS-96. There are some useful pieces of information about what they look forward to about being in space.

Office of University Relations, University of Texas–Pan American, "Latina Day During HESTIC Brings Inspiration to Young Women." www.utpa.edu/news/index.cfm?newsid=2586&cur type=release&curbar=news. This university bulletin contains some excellent material from Ochoa and other important people about the value of education and the role of Hispanics in space.

"Star-Trekking: Ellen Ochoa, PhD." www.womenworking2000. com/feature/index.php?id=81. This short article about Ochoa contains some helpful comments on her shuttle flights and on the impact she has made on females.

Megan Sullivan, "An Interview with NASA Astronaut Ellen Ochoa," *Science Teacher*, February 2005. www.nsta.org/main/news/ stories/science_teacher.php?news_story_ID=50189.

## Web Sites

**Kennedy Space Center.** http://science.ksc.nasa.gov. This site provides links to summaries of shuttle flights, including those by Ellen Ochoa. Students can also find more information on flight crews, missions, and their outcomes.

**National Aeronatautics and Space Administration (NASA).** http://spaceflight.nasa.gov/shuttle. This site provides links to interviews with space shuttle crew members, including Ellen Ochoa. It also includes links to background on individual astronauts and to information about the space shuttle and its many missions.

# Index

# Picture Credits

# About the Author

John F. Wukovits is a retired junior high school teacher and writer from Trenton, Michigan, who specializes in history and biography. Besides biographies of Anne Frank, Jim Carrey, Michael J. Fox, Stephen King, and Martin Luther King Jr. for Lucent, he has written biographies of the World War II commander Admiral Clifton Sprague, Barry Sanders, Tim Allen, Jack Nicklaus, Vince Lombardi, and Wyatt Earp. He is also the author of many books about World War II, including the July 2003 book *Pacific Alamo: The Battle for Wake Island*, the August 2006 *One Square Mile of Hell: The Battle for Tarawa*, and the November 2006 *Eisenhower: A Biography*. A graduate of the University of Notre Dame, Wukovits has three daughters—Amy, Julie, and Karen—and three grandchildren—Matthew, Megan, and Emma.